MW01284257

Beyond Survival

Beyond Survival

How Judaism Can Thrive in the 21st Century

Terry Bookman

ROWMAN & LITTLEFIELD
Lanham · Boulder · New York · London

Published by Rowman & Littlefield
An imprint of The Rowman & Littlefield Publishing Group, Inc.
4501 Forbes Boulevard, Suite 200, Lanham, Maryland 20706
www.rowman.com

6 Tinworth Street, London SE11 5AL, United Kingdom

Copyright © 2019 by The Rowman & Littlefield Publishing Group, Inc.

All rights reserved. No part of this book may be reproduced in any form or by
any electronic or mechanical means, including information storage and retrieval
systems, without written permission from the publisher, except by a reviewer who
may quote passages in a review.

British Library Cataloguing in Publication Information Available

Library of Congress Cataloging-in-Publication Data

Names: Bookman, Terry, author.
Title: Beyond survival : how Judaism can thrive in the 21st century / Terry Bookman.
Description: Lanham ; Boulder ; New York ; London : Rowman & Littlefield, [2019] |
    Includes bibliographical references and index.
Identifiers: LCCN 2018055316 (print) | LCCN 2018055667 (ebook) | ISBN
    9781538122334 (ebook) | ISBN 9781538122327 (cloth : alk. paper)
Subjects: LCSH: Jews—Identity. | Jews—Civilization. | Judaism—21st century.
Classification: LCC DS143 (ebook) | LCC DS143 .B68 2019 (print) | DDC
    305.892/4—dc23
LC record available at https://lccn.loc.gov/2018055316

∞™ The paper used in this publication meets the minimum requirements of American
National Standard for Information Sciences—Permanence of Paper for Printed Library
Materials, ANSI/NISO Z39.48-1992.

Printed in the United States of America

Contents

Beyond Survival

A New Jewish Vision

$\mathcal{I}$n his latest novel, *Here I Am*, Jonathan Safran Foer writes,

> Survival has been the central theme of Jewish existence since the beginning, and not because we chose it to be that way. We have always had enemies, always been hunted. It's not true that everyone hates Jews, but in every country we've ever lived, in every decade of every century, we have encountered hatred. . . . We are a traumatized people. And nothing else has trauma's power to deform the mind and heart.[1]

I believe this assessment is quite accurate. We Jews have become the world's experts on how to survive. Beginning with the pharaoh of Egypt, immortalized in our retelling of the story at every Passover *seder*, there have been numerous genocidal attempts to eliminate our people from the face of the earth and the annals of history. All have failed. We are still here. And those who attempted to destroy us are gone, their names all but erased from human history. To paraphrase the familiar trope, "survival is our middle name." Even the Dalai Lama, when faced with the reality that his people would be in exile from Tibet for an undetermined amount of time, sought the counsel of numerous Jewish leaders. "'We always talk of the Jewish people scattered in so many countries, speaking so many languages,' the Dalai Lama said in English, sometimes seeking the right word from a Tibetan translator. 'Yet the Jews keep their traditions. It is something very admirable.'" In essence, he "wanted to learn" our "'secret technique' of survival."[2] And yet, survival has come at enormous cost to our collective psyche.

But what if this is a moment in time that calls for a different "skill" or a different "muscle"? With the burgeoning of interest in Judaism, with the recently revealed 2014 Pew Commission finding that Judaism is the most favorably viewed religion in the United States, with the strides Israel has taken to become a world economic, scientific, technological, medical, and military power, as well as one of the world's most popular tourist destinations, is it time for a major paradigm shift, a change of narrative, one that will take us beyond survival to truly thriving?* We who have learned the art of surviving any and all circumstances now have an opportunity to thrive. Can we seize the moment? Are we capable of accepting this new possibility, this new identity? Can the world's number one expert survivalists now embrace thriving? Thus far, call it suspicion or centuries of experience, with rare historical exceptions, we have done a terrible job at thriving. That muscle either does not currently exist or is so severely underdeveloped that we do not know how to use it. But today there is a new reality. We Jews need to get that in almost every place we live, we enjoy privileged status.

We know how to protect ourselves from those would-be haters; how to circle the proverbial wagons and keep "them" out while we make the center strong and safe; and even how to turn their pejoratives into a badge of honor. When they called us "bookish," we prided ourselves on our intellectual acumen. When they called us "cheap money grubbers," we became generous philanthropists. But what if they love us as well as our children? What if they see marrying into our families as a good thing? What if they want to build world-class Jewish studies departments and, instead of quotas to keep us out, recruit as many of our kids as possible? This is not merely a hypothetical. Some years ago, I believe it was 2002, while attending the Union of Reform Judaism's biennial meeting, I took

---

*A recent television campaign for Israeli tourism features a beautiful actress walking the streets of Tel Aviv and Jerusalem with the tagline, "Israel: Beyond Belief." The message is quite clear. No longer is Israel merely appealing to Jewish tourists in the Diaspora to visit the holy places, to connect with their people and heritage. Nor is Israel playing on Jewish guilt for "living the good life" while their coreligionists struggle each day against their enemies just to stay alive. Quite the contrary, it is reaching out to all people with its message that visiting Israel is not limited to having an emotional or religious experience. Rather, Israel is a sexy destination with universal appeal.

some time to see the vendors and information booths, which is one of my favorite things to do at this gathering. All right, I was shopping as well! Imagine my surprise when the very first booth, usually the most expensive one as well, was Vanderbilt University, announcing the launch of its new Jewish Studies Department! Vanderbilt, that bastion of southern gentility, was actively recruiting Jewish students. Its founders must have been rolling in their graves, yet today there is a large and active Jewish student population and a wonderful, world-class library as well. One can even major in Jewish and Holocaust studies. Now Vanderbilt is considered one of the best places for Jewish kids to go to college. Who would have "thunk" it?

In the 2016 American presidential election, both candidates boasted of their Jewish in-law sons and their grandchildren who were being raised as Jews. And, significantly, it was no big deal! It was hardly talked about in any news outlet. And as for Bernie Sanders, if not for an occasional question from the press, the fact that he was a Jew was rarely mentioned—a total nonissue. As a child of the 1960s, I remember when John F. Kennedy was running for president, and his "loyalty to our nation" was questioned because he was a Catholic. Joe Lieberman as a vice presidential candidate was a source of pride for the Jewish community, though the "dual loyalties" question was invoked.* This time? Normal! The times, they have changed. Can we adapt to this new reality?

The common historical perception of the Jewish people (announced in the Torah and bolstered in large measure by the Holocaust) is that our two thousand years of Diaspora has been one of exile, suffering, and persecution. Indeed, we Jews have been oppressed. Our very existence too often rode on the whims and economic fortunes of despotic leaders. Yet, a truer examination of our history would highlight notable examples of our people's capacity to truly thrive. After all, before the expulsion we called our experience "The Golden Age of Spain." Our people thrived for centu-

---

*In the August 12, 2000, issue of the *Los Angeles Times*, the question of Joe Lieberman's loyalty to the United States was indeed raised by none other than Louis Farrakhan. He was reported to have said, "Mr. Lieberman, as an Orthodox Jew, is also a dual citizen of Israel. The state of Israel is not synonymous with the United States, and the test he would probably have to pass is: Would he be more faithful to the Constitution of the United States than to the ties that any Jewish person would have to the state of Israel?" The fact that this question was raised by a fringe individual demonstrates how marginalized the suspicion has become. And the fact that Mr. Farrakhan was mistaken as to Joe Lieberman's "dual" citizenship made it seem all the more ridiculous and out of line.

ries in Babylonia, Germany, and Amsterdam, making timeless contributions to our collective culture and history. The Babylonian Talmud, the poetry and liturgy of our prayer book, the great *Yeshiva* (literally, "place of sitting," but for all intents and purposes, simply a "school") academies, the mystical tradition of *Kabbalah* (literally, "received," the term used for the collective mystical tradition in Judaism), the exploration of the Americas are just a few. In other words, when circumstances and the opportunity present itself, we know how to get beyond survival. The thesis of this book is that now is such a time.

Please allow me, then, to sketch a portrait of what "thriving" might look like for us. Back in the 1990s, I consulted with a synagogue whose members had a reputation for having a kind of snobbish and go-it-alone attitude in the community. When I pointed out that their exit sign read "Do Not Enter," they did not believe me. Even when I led them on a mini field trip to see the sign, they were in denial. And, in fact, it took them another five years to change the sign!

So the very first thing the Jewish community needs to do is take down the invisible (but keenly felt) Do Not Enter sign. We have to lose the language of exclusivity—terms like *"goy"* and *"shikse,"* even "non-Jew"—and make *keruv* (the imperative of reaching out to others) a top priority, becoming a truly welcoming address. Members of a thriving community create numerous low-barrier access points and make sure to warmly greet and attend to newcomers. Whenever practical, they follow up with those same newcomers with openness and curiosity. People in thriving communities are confident in what they provide and are not afraid of "giving it away." They do not talk about joining and how much it will cost; they allow people to join in and later let them ask about how they can support what "we" are doing. Members of thriving communities are confident in taking it out of the building or off campus. They partake in community-wide efforts, talk about "us" and "we" and make sure that the "us" and "we" are diverse. They lovingly support the journeys of others and do not get hurt by or jealous of the choices people make. They do not act out of fear or anger; rather, their actions come from a place of love, openness, compassion, empathy, and understanding. Their agenda is a positive one focused on what they can create and build together, not what they have to defend against. And while members of thriving communities remember the past, they don't dwell on it; rather, they imagine a future even better and brighter than the present. In short, thriving communities are places we want to spend more time in, not because we have to, not out of guilt or even obligation, but because we find them supportive and nourishing, places in which we give of ourselves and get much in return. A thriving community is one I want to live in and would never think of leaving.

During my tenure in Milwaukee (1984–1995), I was speaking at a Unitarian church one Sunday morning. I remembered the old joke that in some communities it had to be called the "Jewnitarian" church because so many Jews who left our faith behind found it to be a welcoming place. When it came time for the announcements, I found out just why. The pastor began by welcoming visitors and new members. She said,

> Today we want to say hello to our dear friend, Cristina, who has returned to our fellowship with her fiancé, Sam Cohen. Sam is of the Jewish faith, our brother, and we are so pleased that he has joined us today. [Applause from the congregation.] We look forward to sharing with Sam and Cristina as they join their lives together next month and to deepening our relationship with both of them. [More applause.]

Okay, I thought it might be a little embarrassing to be noticed in that way. But once I got over that I began to consider what just happened. Can you imagine a similar announcement in a synagogue? One in which the rabbi is genuinely happy that a member is about to marry their other faith partner and is excited that they have come on Shabbat to share in worship? That is a far cry from too many synagogues that will not even wish the parents a *mazal tov* when their children get engaged to a person of another faith.

Time has three components—past, present, and future. The *past* is a series of events and the "stories" we tell about it. By the word "story," I do not mean fiction; rather, I mean a narrative based on our experience and our personal memories of that moment in time—what it meant at the time or still means to us and our lives. When we talk about our past, whether as an individual or a community, we do not tell everything that ever happened. We cannot. Some of it we simply do not remember, a problem many of us experience especially as we age. Some of it we deem irrelevant. And some we have decided is definitive of who we are. We *all* have selective memories. The brain edits all of our experiences. That is part of the human condition. I remember my beloved grandpa, Max, repeating the same stories again and again, each time with the same gusto as if it was the first time. It used to drive my mother crazy, but I loved hearing him tell it. The word "history" can be divided into two words, "his" and "story," which reminds us that even the most deliberate and careful historian is inevitably selective in the data he or she chooses to interpret. That is what we call the past. And in a later chapter, I will discuss what it means to truly remember the collective past for the Jewish community.

The *present* is simply this moment in time as well as the particular filters we are using to analyze what we are experiencing. In a real way, each of us is a filter or a group of filters (created by our DNA and our life experiences) through which we encounter the world. Or as the Talmud states, "We do not see the world as it is; we see the world as we are." In other words, the world—every experience and every person we encounter—occurs to us in a particular way. We live in an "occurring world." We need to realize that it is not the same for everyone else. It may not even be the same for anyone else. There is no getting around that. And while we know that sometimes others may agree with us, we also know that there are still people in this world who insist the earth is flat. Don't try to convince them otherwise.

Finally, there is the *future*. Or is there? We act as if the future exists and that it has definitive shape and form. I am not saying we shouldn't. When I was growing up, my dad had a friend who was convinced the world would be imminently destroyed by a nuclear war. There was no use in having a career or raising a family. He died a very lonely and bitter man. On the other hand, though we all act as if it truly exists, there really is no such thing as a tangible future, at least not one that we can all point to.

So what is the future? It is a time we imagine or envision. In fact, life would be pretty unbearable if we did not. Now some of us project a "for sure" future. Those who do, however, are merely assessing the present (perhaps tempered by the past) and are predicting that if current trends persist and nothing changes, the future will look a lot like the present. They are probably correct. Their collective *imagined future* is bleak, even dystopian, and they are, in effect, living as if it is inevitable. They imagine a future of mere survival, and all are doing their best to be the last one standing.

The worldwide Jewish community has been living under the illusion that we are a people in numerical decline, as if that is inevitable and indisputable. They remind us that we are the only community that has not recovered its losses from the Holocaust in World War II. They cite that Jewish couples are marrying later in life, having fewer children— one or two being the new normal, with many opting out altogether. They cite the intermarriage rate, which has continued unabated for the past fifty years now, to be around 50 percent. It is probably more like 70 percent among the non-Orthodox, which continues to be the over-whelming majority everywhere, even in Israel. They remind us that we are an aging community and that even though thousands join our ranks each year, an equal number drop out for another spiritual path. And they point to the increasing number of synagogue and day school clos-ings and mergers, as well as the decreasing number of donors to Jewish causes, as a sure indication of Jewish apathy or worse. When projected into the future, the numbers look bad as we shrink from numerical in-significance to absolute irrelevancy.

I agree. If we only look at today's trends and project them into the future, the picture is indeed bleak. After all, numbers don't lie. But the future is not simply a matter of assessing the present and pushing it outward. The future does not exist "out there." The future only exists in our imagination. What truly lies ahead, no one knows. Of course, our imagination has to have some basis in reality. But being "realistic" is often just a cop-out for maintaining the status quo, for doing things the way we always have.

I am reminded of the book *Who Moved My Cheese?* by Spencer John-son.[3] In this allegorical tale, each day the mice receive their daily ration of cheese. Where it comes from, they do not know, but that is the way it has always been, as every mouse knows. This is their sure reality. Then one day, the cheese fails to appear. Of course there is some grumbling and concern, but they manage to do without. However, this continues day after day. No cheese. Eventually, some of the mice venture out and find there is cheese elsewhere. But many refuse to leave, insisting that the cheese will reappear. And they do so until they perish. The parable is clear. The mantra "we have always done it this way," which exists in too many organizations, is a prescription for decline and destruction. You don't have to take my word for it. Just look at any thriving organization, Jewish or otherwise. I guarantee they are not relying on the past to get them to the future; rather, they are preserving what is best from their past and innovating, creating their desired future.

Nor are they paralyzed by fear. We learn from neuroscience that we have an emotion dedicated to recognizing and focusing on threats—fear. It is a survival mechanism, putting us on high alert when any potential danger is near. However, there is a downside: our brains have an inherent "better safe than sorry" approach, which means that we regularly experience fear in situations where it's not really warranted.[4] Fear limits us. Just think of the posture of fear—a person crouching or hiding. Nothing can be created out of such a space. The best that can happen is nothing. And in today's fast-paced, ever-changing world, doing nothing means moving backward. Afraid of losing what we have, of alienating the base that has supported us for decades, the Jewish community is in lockdown mode, even as we watch the decline in the Diaspora and the isolation in Israel, which is now accelerating.

The organized Jewish establishment seems quite resigned in this matter. Resignation is what happens to us when we lose all hope, when our vision is blocked, and when we cannot see beyond the immediate reality that appears dystopian and dark. I have a committed Jewish friend who told me recently that he watches Christian pastors like Joel Osteen on television not because he is having a crisis in faith. He watches them because they have a positive, optimistic view of the world. While they recognize we all sin and fail, they see people with unlimited capacity to grow and do the right thing. They believe in God and they believe in us. These Christian pastors serve as an antidote to the gloom and doom he hears from his rabbi and from the Jewish community as a whole. Ironically, these Christian pastors restore his hope in his Jewish faith!

So what if, instead of imagining a future in which there are only half the number of Jews that we have today, we imagine a future with twice as many? Can you picture a worldwide Jewish community of thirty million people? I can. And the good news is it will not be all that difficult to achieve. Right now, the worldwide Jewish community is predicting a future of continued decline. We are preparing for that future by downsizing our institutional infrastructure. Synagogues are merging, day schools are shutting down, and national organizations are cutting staff, limiting space, or eliminating services altogether. All are looking at current numbers, seeing the trends, and assuming nothing will change.

But what if we imagine a different future? One in which the Jewish people are thriving? For sure, that future will look a lot different from the Jewish present. The narratives we love to tell about how everyone always hates us and we cannot trust them will have to change. And we as a people will look a lot different as well. This book is about that future, a future of thriving instead of mere survival. Each chapter will describe a different obstacle, challenge, opportunity, or task confronting us and what we can do about it. Some will inevitably say that I am not being realistic. Of course I am not. Nothing great has ever happened in this world by being realistic. "Realistic" is a survival word. Was Reverend Martin Luther King Jr. being realistic in 1963 when he said, "I have a dream"? He dreamed of a radically different future for his people, for all of us. And today it is reality. As a people, we will have to develop different "muscles" in order to thrive. But I believe in us and I believe we can. Are you ready to thrive?

Part I

OBSTACLES

· 1 ·

The Big Three Plus One

𝒻or more than a half century, three issues have preoccupied the consciousness, motivated the actions, and garnered the lion's share of the fundraising dollars of the Jewish people: anti-Semitism, the Holocaust, and the precariousness of the State of Israel. The plus one, often implied in these three, is combatting assimilation. Collectively, these four "realities" have comprised the bulk of our community's survivalist agenda, and as a people, we have "waxed fat" on our many successes.* Now while I admit that all of these need to stay on our communal agenda, and recognizing what I am about to say will sound like anathema to just about anyone in the Jewish establishment, the reality is they are no longer the central issues of Jewish life and identity, especially for anyone under the age of forty. When we speak to young people, they have no personal experience with anti-Semitism; it is something that happened to their grandparents. The Holocaust sounds like ancient history to them. And the only Israel they know is a nation that is vibrant and strong. That is why we need to—in fact, we must—go "beyond survival."

To accept this new reality—this new paradigm—the Jewish community, including the synagogue world, will have to radically change its message while reinvesting its time and commitment to new core priorities.† We will need to let go of the very things that gave us meaning and

---

*The Bible uses the term "waxed fat" as a metaphor for complacency, ethical lapse, moral decline, and faithlessness. I have employed it here with similar connotations.

† A paradigm is a mental construct through which we see reality. Change occurs when we shift things around or replace some things with new ones. A paradigm shift, on the

purpose, and that made us strong, so that we can embrace the numerous opportunities to thrive that are uniquely presenting themselves for the first time in our people's history. In the process, we will need to shift alliances, making new friends and allies and creating new coalitions rooted in shared values. In a way, we will need to let go of all that is familiar so that we can create a future once unimaginable, but which is now at our fingertips. We will need to summon a courage long dormant, but in the very DNA of our people—the courage of an Avram and Sarai, our founding parents, who left behind almost everything they knew to follow a dream, transforming their lives and changing the world; the courage of a slave people who defied their Egyptian captors to traverse a harsh and unknown wilderness to a Land only known through a centuries-old Promise; the courage of generations exiled from their land, with rabbis who redefined our faith from Temple to synagogue, creating academies that kept Jewish learning and living alive; the courage of millions who left their homes in Spain rather than lose their faith as well as those who kept their faith alive in secret; the courage of our *chalutzim*, the very first "pioneers" who came back to our Land clearing it of swamps while planting forests, armed only with the hope and a dream of our people's collective return; or the courage of a trapped people who defied their Nazi captors in the Warsaw ghetto uprising, and the partisans in the forests of Europe. Each of these "moments in courage" represents a paradigm shift for the Jewish people, when "business as usual" was no longer useful or productive. With that same courage mixed with imagination, we can, we must, we will let go of the Big Three and thrive.

ANTI-SEMITISM

I am convinced that as long as there is a single Jew in the world, there will be at least one anti-Semite—a sad, but true commentary on the dark side of human nature. (Similarly, as long as there are people with dark skin

---

other hand, is when we change the very construct out of which we have created our reality. While change, which inevitably signals loss, is never easy—we grow attached to things and ideas even when they are no longer operative or even useful (check your garage/basement/attic/closets if you don't believe me)—a paradigm shift is monumental, requiring vision, will, energy, courage, and resources.

there will be racists; as long as there are women, there will be misogynists; and as long as there are homosexuals, there will be homophobes to fear and hate them.) At the same time, take a deep breath; despite what you may read or see in the news, in most of the world, the scourge that was anti-Semitism no longer exists. It is over. Gone. Let me explain.

An anti-Semite is a person who has a nonrational antipathy or even hatred of Jews. That is to say, this person, often buoyed by some pseudo-science or half-baked conspiracy theory, believes that Jews are a subspecies of human beings, Christ killers, bent on world domination through control of international finance and the media. Like all prejudice, it is based on an exaggeration of the truth resulting in stereotypes that are transferred to any and all people in that category. Like all prejudice, it is pernicious, filled with hate speech often leading to hateful acts of violence and destruction, or even worse, the taking of human life. It does not take a rocket scientist to realize there are all sorts of anti-Semites alive and well in our world, even growing in numbers as part of the resurging far Right in Europe. Though most (but not all) of them are undereducated, underemployed, angry, and insecure "losers," their words and actions must be taken seriously and monitored continuously.[1] Fortunately, in North America, we have excellent organizations like the Anti-Defamation League and the Southern Poverty Law Center to do this important work on our behalf. Unfortunately, as we see rather regularly in our news these days, and most recently (at the time of this writing) in Pittsburgh, it only takes one hater to wreak untold tragedy in the lives of decent, law-abiding, positive citizens of the world. And as I just wrote, there is absolutely no way to eliminate all the anti-Semites in society. No amount of education or rational convincing will talk these people out of the false "truth" in which they believe. We may have had that fantasy in the nineteenth century that the inevitable "perfection of man" would come about through universal education and economic prosperity, but the twentieth century, the bloodiest in human history, has sadly shown us differently.*

*Coming out of the so-called Age of Enlightenment, the world was filled with optimism that we could create the perfect society and eliminate all human failing and shortcomings. Whether it was through a religious lens or one of the many secular "isms," we believed that with the "right system" we were heading toward utopia. World War I, then dubbed "the war to end all wars" was a wake-up call that such belief was, to say the least, premature. Unfortunately, we did not heed the alarm. It took another World War, the scientific and systematic murder of millions of "undesirables," two atomic bombs

Anti-Semitism, on the other hand, is something much worse. As I write this, we are still reeling from the spate of violence perpetrated by the neo-Nazis and Ku Klux Klan sympathizers in Charlottesville, Virginia. To be honest, I was both frightened and disgusted by their marching with torches and their hateful chants. But what happened there, and the immediate aftermath, is quite instructive. As these so-called white supremacists gathered to demonstrate their ugly hatred, even more people gathered to counter-demonstrate, a trend that has continued all over the world. And after one of their number took his car to murder those who stood for love and equality and tragically succeeded in taking the life of a caring young woman, Heather Heyer, all across America people marched against senseless hatred while the news media as well as political leaders and police forces decried that there is no place in our world for these anti-Semites and racists! The outpouring of support for Jews and Americans of color was truly overwhelming. For example, after the Pittsburgh synagogue shootings in 2018, the *Pittsburgh Post-Gazette*'s unprecedented headline included an actual quote from the Jewish mourner's *Kaddish* prayer, and the local Muslim community showed compassion by raising money to help the victims!

In a world in which there is true anti-Semitism, the white supremacists not only would have been applauded and condoned (as they were by our president, Donald Trump) but also would have been protected by the authorities. In fact, they may have acted on behalf of those in power. Anti-Semitism exists when the prejudice is embedded in the laws and culture of the land, when discrimination and quotas are legal and a blind eye is turned toward the victims who have no recourse except to suffer the abuse and violence perpetrated upon them (or escape to another country that will protect them, if one exists).

We Jews know real anti-Semitism. We have faced this scar on society as well as humanity for much of our history, especially in Europe and even in the great democracy of the United States. Often we cowered and tried not to make waves, hoping we could just get through it unscathed. Fortu-

---

dropped on civilians, a Cold War with the threat of worldwide nuclear destruction, plus numerous other wars and genocides to get us to finally understand that we were not there yet. From a Jewish religious perspective, the "there" can only be reached in the time of the Messiah, either when the anointed one shows up for the first time (Jewish belief) or upon the return (Christian belief).

nately, through our collective grit and determination, we survived, doing the best we could. After all, where could we go? And so now—when the laws and the authorities actually protect us; when anti-Semitic acts are labeled "hate crimes" and are prosecuted to the full extent of the law; when leaders of all faiths and all walks of life speak out in our behalf; and when neo-Nazi ideology in all its varieties has been repudiated in most of the civilized world—we should be celebrating. Instead, we continue to wring our hands, investing enormous energy and resources in fighting a problem that no longer exists, pointing to the increase in sporadic anti-Semitic acts as evidence that we are once again (or still?) in trouble. In fact, like the paranoid character in a Woody Allen film who heard the word "Jew" when the person who had passed him on the street said, "you," we continue to pump up the actions of every crazy anti-Semite as proof that we need to be hyper vigilant against the age-old problem that fortunately no longer plagues us. I am not even for a moment suggesting we ignore the individual haters or their actions. Let us prosecute them to the full extent of the law. But let us call it what it truly is—the actions of anti-Semites, *not* anti-Semitism!

A cynic might say that these Jewish leaders and organizations created to fight and safeguard us against anti-Semitism are artificially keeping this issue alive in order to maintain their large budgets and powerful status in the Jewish and American establishment. After all, the famed sociologist Max Weber, whose definition of power in society has remained the starting point for many sociologists, warns us that bureaucracies can become a kind of self-sustaining "iron cage" stifling creativity as well as individual freedom.[2] Personally, I prefer not to go that route. The Jewish people have been persecuted for so long that many of us continue to see the world as "out to get us." Every word or action aimed against us, even legitimate critique, becomes proof that anti-Semitism is alive and well. That is just how the world occurs to them. And so they play the "best" tool in their arsenal—and the anti-Semitism card.

I understand that for some of those who lived through decades of real prejudice, including violence aimed against them simply because they were Jews, this may never change. But a younger millennial generation—who has not personally experienced anti-Semitism, who has been called the most diverse generation in American history, and whose friends, lovers, and business associates come from all walks of life—sees a very different world. For them, the world is wide open and inviting, with every opportunity awaiting them. Instead of trying to convince them that they are young and foolish, that anti-Semitism is lurking right around the corner out to get them, we will need to adjust our communal agenda to this new reality, one that works with our authorities to help protect us from and prosecute all forms of hate crimes but, at the same time, celebrates our hard-won status, saving our precious resources to build (not merely protect) our community.

THE HOLOCAUST

The contemporary Jewish philosopher Emil Fackenheim famously stated that in our own time a 614th commandment must be added to God's expectations of us—to remember the Holocaust. Though our people's history is replete with numerous attempts to destroy us, this act of genocide on the part of the Nazis in World War II was so heinous, so unique, that a new word—*Shoa*—was added to our vocabulary, and a separate day of remembrance was added to our Jewish calendar (though some in our community add the *Shoa* to the already established day to remember the disastrous destruction of our Temples in Jerusalem and our subsequent exile, *Tisha b'Av*).* Though a theological debate over the place of the Holocaust continues—whether this was the "logical" outcome of centuries of hatred toward our people or an anomalous, one-time aberration perpetrated by a madman—no one in the Jewish world would deny its impact on our collective psyche or our communal need to remember and to pass down those lessons to our children and our children's children. Today, with the number of eyewitnesses diminishing with every passing year, that imperative becomes all the more important. As William Faulkner famously wrote, "The past is never dead. It's not even past."[3]

---

*I remember having an audience with the Dalai Lama together with my rabbinic colleagues. Speaking through a translator, he demonstrated great empathy and compassion toward the Jewish people. When attempting to reference the Holocaust, he struggled to find the correct word in his native language but, in the end, could not. Tears flowed down my face for the shame I felt at the moment being a part of so-called Western civilization and how often we in the West flaunt our superiority over people of color throughout the developing world.

And we have done an excellent job. Holocaust museums and memorials exist in numerous cities around the world. Thousands of books have been written on the subject. Holocaust studies have entered the curriculum of schools and universities, even as a major. And though Holocaust deniers continue in their malicious attempts to debunk historical reality, the vast majority of people of good will own the horrors perpetrated upon our people as well as other innocent noncombatant groups (e.g., the Roma, homosexuals, communists, and the disabled) who perished during the nightmare created by Hitler, the German people, and their collaborators. Perhaps ironically nowhere is this more evident than in modern-day Germany itself, where even the public display of Nazi symbols is against the law.

Still, though we are not permitted to forget, is it enough merely to remember? We are the creators of the expression, "Never Again," but what do we really mean by these words? Have they, in fact, become an empty slogan? After all, since the Holocaust there have been other attempts at genocide perpetrated in Rwanda and Cambodia, just to name two. And by the way, when visiting the Holocaust Museum in Kigali, Rwanda, I was incredibly moved by the fact that this tiny house included all the other modern-day inhumanities, including our own. We need to ask ourselves this difficult question: Does "Never Again" only apply to the Jewish people? Is that the community we want to be?

We Jews are a remembering people. We remember our enslavement in Egypt as a moral imperative to take care of the poor and the powerless, to never oppress others, to free our fellows from the horrors of hunger and homelessness, and to raise our voices against all forms of tyranny wherever it may occur. Our track record in this regard is pretty solid. Throughout the centuries, Jewish people have been leaders in all aspects of social justice crusades and causes for the betterment of humanity. We should take collective pride in all that we have done to make the world a better place, even as we commit ourselves to that sacred purpose in every generation.

We remember our loved ones with *Yizkor* (literally, "He will remember," a memorial service within the larger *Shacharit*/morning worship service) four times a year and annually on the date of their *yahrtzeit* (the Yiddish word for "anniversary of decease," the day one died). We have added a day to our calendar, *Yom haZikaron*, a day to remember all those soldiers and civilians who have died in the defense of our collective Homeland,

Israel. During the sacred holy day of *Rosh haShanah*, one section of the shofar service called *Zichronot* is dedicated to memory as we recall our own misdeeds of the previous year. Every worship service includes the *Kaddish* prayer as we pray for our family members who have passed away during the previous year. It was the founder of modern-day Hasidism, the Ba'al Shem Tov, who reminded us that "forgetfulness leads to exile; remembrance is the secret of redemption."[4]

Likewise, we Jews must always remember the Holocaust. After all, one-third of our people were brutally murdered—wiped off the face of the earth for the "crime" of being born Jewish. One-and-a-half million children, taken from their parents, were denied the opportunity to grow up and make their mark on the world. As a parent, I cannot even imagine the horror of losing my child in this way. But the lessons of the Holocaust must be more than a "family memory." If the Holocaust becomes a "poor us, we always suffer, the world is out to get us" victim-type message, it may strengthen us for a while but will be bound to fade into the annals of Jewish history. In fact, in a provocative interview on NPR after the release of his book, *The Holocaust Is Over: We Must Rise from Its Ashes*, Avraham Burg suggests that Israel has been so influenced by the horrors of the Holocaust that the nation has lost its ability to trust, leading to a growing nationalism and violence that hinders peace in the region. He challenges his fellow citizens that clinging to the tragedies of the past serves to block the path of a more positive future. The wounds inflicted by the Holocaust are still raw because they never healed properly in the first place. It is time we healed. We Jews do not have a monopoly on suffering yet we often act as if we do.[5] This is memory as paralysis, not motivation. However, if the lessons of the Holocaust serve to raise the consciousness of all others, make the world a more caring place, and embolden others to never be silent but instead stand up against injustice, bigotry, and hatred wherever it raises its ugliness, then it will live forever, as it should. It is for this reason that we can never allow the world, which for the most part turned a blind eye, to ever forget, though I am certain many would like to do just that.

Beyond that, we have to acknowledge that memory is always and only about the past. But is it enough to build a future? If all we are about is memory, vowing never to allow history to repeat itself, can that alone sustain the next generation and the ones after that? As the mayor of New Orleans said in defending his city's decision to remove Confederate statues prominently on display, "There is a difference between remembrance of history and reverence of it."[6] History cannot be changed; what is done is done. I would venture to say that as we distance ourselves from any historical event, no matter how significant or powerful, its motivational impact diminishes over time, or is lost entirely. Just look at all the American holidays created to be eternal reminders—Veteran's Day, Labor Day, Flag Day, among others—all of them turned into shopping opportunities after a sparsely attended parade or rally.* Today, more people celebrate Halloween, for goodness sake! Yes, we must remember but in a way that empowers us today. Or as Rabbi Adina Allen wrote, in her attempt to capture this challenge, our task is "to engage the past in a way that welcomes the full reality of the present so that the future may be beautiful beyond our wildest imagination."[7]

ISRAEL

Have you ever been on a Birthright trip to Israel? Do you know a young adult who has? According to the Birthright Israel website, more than 650,000 people from more than sixty-seven countries have done so thus far. In speaking to participants, the number one response I have heard is, "It was amazing, a blast, life-changing . . . can't wait to go back for a longer period of time." They meet soldiers, people their own age, investigate career matches, shop at cool stores, go to parties, and have fun. For sure, they visit some of the more important historical sites and learn about Israel's history and security issues, but that is not the focus of the trip. In other words, by far the most successful program introducing the millennial generation to Israel focuses on what a great place Israel is to live, work, and play. Not exactly our *bubbe*'s Israel!

When I was growing up, I remember my mother and grandmother packing up boxes of used clothes to send to our poor cousins in Israel. Wrapped into the clothes were simple medical supplies like Band-Aids and aspirin, as well as cans of foodstuffs like tuna and sardines. Today,

---

*Lest we think this is unique to American culture, when is the last time anyone you know fasted in honor of Gedaliah? While it still remains on the Jewish calendar its relevance is lost on the vast majority of the Jewish world. This occurs in all cultures. We think, at the moment, that the big events impacting our lives will last forever. They don't.

those same cousins look to Milan and Paris for the latest in fashion. Now I am not suggesting that everyone in Israel is well off financially. Far from it. As a modern-day nation with an economy ranked in the top twenty and the ninth most powerful military in the world, Israel suffers from all the same problems that plague every modern industrial capitalist nation—haves and have nots, poverty, drug addiction, and homelessness. On the other hand, any sensible person would take one look at all the construction cranes that dot the landscape and have to agree that Israel is no longer the land of our "poor relations." Yet, the agenda of the organized Jewish community seems to love a Middle East crisis while it continues to promote an insecure Israel that desperately needs our *tzedakah* lest it go under. For quite some time, I have wondered who is really being served by such an approach—Israel itself or the multiple organizations with their huge staffs, powerful political clout, well-intended volunteers and donors, and extraordinary budgets?[8]

This patronizing approach to our brothers and sisters living in the Land of Promise is nothing new. In ancient times, Jews in the Diaspora fought for control over such central issues as the calendar, *halachic*/legal authority, and holy days. In fact, though most Jews are unaware of this fact, there are actually two Talmuds, one written in Babylonia (where the majority of our people lived and prospered, and where the great academies of Sura and Pumpadita were located [the Harvard and Yale of the ancient Jewish world]) and the other (called the *Yerushalmi*) in Palestine, where barely a remnant population kept our connection to the Land alive. The former is the authoritative one, with the latter hardly ever studied in any Jewish hall of higher learning, let alone by lay people. Throughout the centuries of our people's exile, the vast majority of our people lived outside what we now call the Land of Israel. While there is a Torah *mitzvah* to settle in the Land, one that still plays powerfully in the collective consciousness of our people the world over, our rabbis allowed "economic support of those who do" to substitute for this commanded obligation. Apparently two millennia of practice created a habit that is hard to break, or as my cousin from Haifa used to say, "You Americans have given up your birthright for a juicy steak!"

Advocates for the status quo point to all the good work accomplished on behalf of Israel's citizenry through the generosity of those of us in the Diaspora, including hospitals, development towns adopted by cities around the world, schools and *yeshivot* (plural of *yeshivah*, or school with a religious curriculum and agenda), sports programs, and aid to soldiers, as well as hundreds of not-for-profits propped up by Diaspora fundraising. All true. Why wouldn't an Israeli want us to fund their nongovernmental organizations? After all, we are good at it and we have the wealth to do so. Besides, if we did not, they would have to fundraise from a highly taxed population not used to giving, which expects the government will take care of these needs. However, younger Israelis want a new relationship with their cousins abroad—one of equal partners in which there is a true exchange. They want a give-and-take relationship, unlike the one that currently exists—we give and they take. Such a relationship of true mutuality would embrace shared economic partnerships with Israeli talent traveling abroad to teach us a thing or two. Of course, we could not even imagine such a thing in the first decades of the State of Israel struggling for its very survival. Thankfully, those days are really in the past with new business and cultural alliances popping up with regularity. Just look at today's travel ads on television enticing people to come to Israel—sexy women, contemporary music—a "vacation beyond belief!" As I noted earlier, the double entendre should not be lost on any of us.

Recently one of my son's friends decided to live in Israel because he saw greater economic opportunity as well as entry level positions in his chosen field of study than he could realize back home. He spent three years honing his skills before being recruited by an American firm that was impressed by his training. He also spent three years falling in love with Israel, which he now considers his second home. Nor was he alone. Through my kids who made *alliyah* (literally, "going up" or, in other words, "immigration to Israel") and served in the Israel Defense Forces, I have met dozens of young American, French, Australian, English, and Latin American Jews who sought and found opportunity in Israel. Nor was it limited to members of the tribe. I met young adults from various backgrounds, races, religions, ethnicities, cultures, and countries who came to Israel for the experience and stayed for the lifestyle. And there could be many more if and when Israel learns that not every talented individual with something to contribute to its future has to be Jewish and truly relaxes its immigration policy to allow for this influx. Imagine a true multicultural Israel with friends all over the world! I can. The alternative, an isolated Israel fending off its growing list of enemies and indifferent nations, a "client nation" depending on American largesse, is simply and irrefutably unsustainable.

PLUS ONE

Though we rarely hear the word anymore, the underlying core of the old agenda is assimilation, which is why I have made it the "plus one." After coming to America in the nineteenth and twentieth centuries, for the most part, Jews held fast to their faith, traditions, and people; we lived together, worked together, and married one another's children. However, by the second generation we already began to see slippage as people changed their names, "fixed" their noses, dyed and straightened their hair, and moved out of the city centers to the suburbs and beyond. We spoke English (or Spanish) without an accent. We sent our children to public schools and universities. Many of us brought a "Chanukah bush" into our homes. In short, we became American Jews (or British, French, Australian, etc.) assimilating into the host culture's way of life. Nationality came first.*

Now while some would see this as success, after all, we gained acceptance and opportunity in our new homes, the organized Jewish community labeled this as an egregious "sin," a veritable betrayal of our venerated ancestors. Some still do. "The longstanding angst within the American Jewish community around assimilation, intermarriage and fertility," writes Ross Douthat in the *New York Times*, "tends to sustain a kind of soft traditionalist pressure even in liberal Jewish life."[9] This view not only alienates an entire generation of young people but also demonstrates a shallow understanding of Jewish history. You see, assimilation is not a dirty word; rather, contrary to the pejorative way it is talked about by Jewish leaders, assimilation is the true basis for our survival and growth for more than four millennia. While our people had an uncanny ability to keep the core values and practices of our tradition alive, we have also become experts at picking and choosing the best of our host societies and making it somehow Jewish.

---

*Even in Israel, most citizens describe themselves as "Israelis," not Jews. This is also true in the Arab sector but with less frequency. Nationality holds sway as our primary identity marker.

Just think of Jewish food for a moment. Really, do Jews ever not think of Jewish food? What we call "traditional" (like gefilte fish, *kreplach*, knishes) almost always has its origins in the land and people of the surrounding culture. Even what we have come to know and love as Israeli food (like hummus and falafel) is really the foods of the Middle East. What is true of food is also true of music, art, modes of worship, language, calendar, dress, philosophy, sacred and even legal literature— you name it. There is not a single aspect of Jewish life that has not been influenced by and adapted to its host culture. And what one group of Jews considers its foundational culture, Jews from another part of the world see as completely alien. We Jews are the great assimilators of history! And contrary to the way it is often demonized, we are a better, stronger people because of it.

One important example is feminism. It is clear from all of history that women did not have equal rights and opportunities in the ancient world—not in Judaism, not in just about any known culture. Feminism is a modern movement. Women only won the right to vote in the United States in the twentieth century through the suffragette movement, which ultimately led to an amendment of our Constitution. Not so very long ago, we Americans had to change the very Constitution in order for women to obtain the simple human right of casting a ballot. Most Jews have embraced such a notion, even though it is nowhere found in our tradition. Yes, beginning in the ancient world, Jewish women were respected and protected in ways that were way ahead of other contemporary cultures of the time. We can be rightfully proud of that. But they were not, by any stretch of the imagination, equal. The modern Jewish community assimilated this idea by using the Torah verse from Genesis 1:27, *"Vayivrah Elohim et ha'adam b'tzalmo, b'tzelem Elohim barah o'toe; zachar oo'n'kayvah barah otam"* (In the image of God were they created, male and female) and recasting it as an ideal of gender equality, intrinsic to Judaism itself. Brilliant! Today we have celebration of baby girls entering the covenant, *Bat Mitzvah*, with those same girls chanting Torah, co-equal Jewish education for both genders, and leadership opportunities at every level of Jewish life, both professional and volunteer. And no one thinks of it as assimilation anymore. I call that success! And lest one think this is only true of liberal Jews, consider the Beis Ya'acov school system for Orthodox girls who study the Torah, the Talmud, and Jewish law. There was no such opportunity for females even in my mother's time. Thank-you assimilation!

What is true for the role of women is also true, as stated earlier, of dozens of cultural norms and values that did not have their origins in Judaism, but which have found their way into our way of life. Assimilation is part and parcel of being a human being. Those who assimilate are not traitors, nor are they consciously eschewing their Jewish identity. End of subject.

WHERE DOES THIS LEAVE US?

The Big Three as I have called them in this chapter constitute the past for the Jewish people. And because it is an ongoing reality of life itself, so does the plus one. Sadly, the organized Jewish community is hooked on the past, seemingly unable to let it go. Why is that? Well, in part, memory is a feature of Judaism itself. We are a remembering people. *Yizkor* is not only for saying *Kaddish* for our loved ones; it helps to define who we are today. I am not just Terry Bookman. I am *Tuvyah* son of *Asher* and *Leah*. And *Tuvyah* was the father of my maternal grandfather whose pet name for me was *tata* (Yiddish for father) . . . and so it goes. That's a good thing.

But it is more than that. If we are honest, something I have tried to be throughout the pages of this book, we have to admit that the Big Three served to animate our parents' generation. It gave them a focus. For the most part, they were not a particularly religious generation (like their parents and grandparents were), but they were fiercely and proudly Jewish in their identity. And so a generation of good people could work together to keep Judaism alive without having to do much that was ritually or observably Jewish. Without even a hint of ambivalence, they could be Jews, staving off the outside world, fighting the good fight, raising money and awareness, making sure Israel was strong, creating opportunity for their children, and keeping us safe. And that was enough for them. We must be grateful for all that they were able to accomplish. The Jewish institutions they created formed the backbone and strength of our community. And we have a State of Israel that has made us proud more times than we can count.*

---

*I always hate it when Jews refer to themselves as "once-a-year Jews" because they only attend worship services during the High Holy Days. I am quick to point out to them all

Nevertheless, the past is a memory, not an agenda. Our parents and grandparents may have very well saved the Jewish people, but, and here is the rub, we do not need saving right now. Instead, we need to thrive and grow. Saving is, in reality, based on a scarcity mentality. A threatened and endangered group must circle the proverbial wagons and fight off the enemy attackers, merely and hopefully just to survive. This they did. And we are here to talk about it. Centuries of attack, both real and perceived, have traumatized our people and, in the process, created a victimhood mentality. What we know about traumatized individuals is that their deep-rooted fears can be triggered with often the slightest provocation. We even have named a psychological condition for this—post-traumatic stress disorder. We Jews suffer from that condition, and it is very difficult to heal. Being a victim brings great sympathy as people feel sorry for one's suffering. But it also weakens us, places us in a situation in which we do not have to take responsibility for our pain. The other thing about victimhood is that it is self-corroborating, even self-perpetuating. Everyone is out to get us. And when the synagogue even in another country is defaced, we have all the proof we need that "here it goes again."* While we understand trauma and victimhood, living in it keeps us stuck, frozen in time.

However, today, what we have to fully realize is that the old enemy, in far greater numbers, loves us and lobbies on our behalf. They are our friends, neighbors, coworkers, even our family. They gladly join us in every celebration of life and every holiday. They are a significant part of who we are today. My parents used to say, "Scratch a *goy* and you will find an anti-Semite!" They believed it. Perhaps some in our tribe still do. They are mistaken. Happily so. We Jews must remember the past, but we must never revere it. To do so is to turn it into some kind of idolatry. In many parts of the Jewish world today, to even question the relevance of the Big Three is to be labeled a "heretic," a "self-hating Jew," or "naive and fool-

---

the other Jewish identity markers they embrace, reminding them that being observant of Jewish ritual is only one such marker. It is not the only one!

*We hear a great deal today that "anti-Semitism is on the rise," and it is certainly true that anti-Semitic acts have risen substantially in the last year, which is a cause for concern. However, what we do not hear is that the number of these acts are actually down from the years 1996 to 2008, according to the Jewish Virtual Library (Jewish Virtual Library, "Anti-Semitism in the United States: Statistics on Religious Hate Crimes," https://www.jewishvirtuallibrary.org/statistics-on-religious-hate-crimes). Such "mistakes" or misrepresentations may have some short-term benefit, but in the long run, they undermine our ability to motivate our brothers and sisters into true action.

ish," and to risk exclusion. We have to be better than that, for if we do not, our children will go elsewhere, just as they did in the 1960s and 1970s when we "exported" Jews who were seeking greater spirituality.*

In short, we need to wean ourselves off the Big Three and, at the same time, recreate and recast all our communal institutions to reflect the new reality, like HIAS (the Hebrew Immigrant Aid Society) did by recasting its mission from aiding refugees who were Jews to aiding *all* refugees because *we* are Jews! This may mean that some institutions will have to shut down, or go "out of business," so to speak.† So be it. We need to provide this generation with positive reasons to be Jewish, ones that will enhance and even transform their lives for the better—a Judaism that truly thrives, not merely survives.

---

*An apocryphal story that has made the rounds in the Jewish world goes something like this: A Zen master once told a rabbi, "The Jewish people are the most spiritual people in the world!" When the rabbi asked, "Why do you say that?" the Roshi replied, "Wherever I travel to ashrams and monasteries they are filled with Jews!" Unfortunately, when Jews sought a more spiritual synagogue experience they were made to feel like weirdos or outsiders, even though there is a rich tradition of meditation practice and mysticism safely within the bounds of our tradition. So they left and went outside the community. How many still do?

† I was once asked in an interview what I would do to save Reform Judaism from its current decline. I replied, "Do you mean save the foundational institutions like the URJ [Union for Reform Judaism], HUC-JIR [Hebrew Union College–Jewish Institute of Religion], and the CCAR [Central Conference of American Rabbis] or save the founding principle, which is Reform, and which existed prior to these organizations?" My question ended the interview. By contrast, when I was growing up, we used to put dimes in a card that was almost ubiquitous in every store for the March of Dimes, a wonderful charity created to fight against childhood polio. In the early 1970s, when they realized they had been successful in their mission, they faced the choice of shutting down or recreating themselves into something new. They did the latter, taking on a new mission to cure all other childhood illnesses as well as birth defects and premature infant mortality. They continue to thrive today.

An Ugly Truth

*T*here is an ugly truth that the organized Jewish community does not like to talk about. In every major community worldwide, including Israel, both the political and economic power is primarily held by Ashkenazim, descendants of Jews from Northern and Western Europe. In the early days of the modern State of Israel, both Sephardic and Mizrachi Jews from North Africa as well as the Middle East were mistreated and misled; they also faced discrimination. Newly arrived immigrants from these parts of the world, and later from Ethiopia, were often sent to so-called development towns or *ma'aborot* (squalid tent cities) mired in poverty, poor education, and lack of access. Their cultures and way of life were denigrated. They were thought of as ignorant and primitive. Upon arrival in Israel, they were humiliated when Israeli immigration authorities shaved their heads and sprayed their bodies with the pesticide DDT. Later, enforced secularization, the destruction of traditional family structures, the "kidnapping or selling" of their babies for adoption, and the reduced status of the patriarch all led to decades of impoverishment and feelings of social inferiority.* Whether or not Jewish leaders in the

---

*Israeli journalist Yael Tzadok who has investigated this tragedy dubbed it "Israel's darkest secret." While it is now known as the "Yemenite Children Affair," the truth is that thousands of babies from Iraq, Morocco, Tunisia, and the Balkans were "stolen" from their parents (who were told their baby died) and given up for adoption to Ashkenazi parents, many of whom had lost children in the Holocaust. When the birth parents asked to see the grave, they were told it was not permitted. Such inhumane treatment was justified by Israel's leadership (including its first prime minister, David Ben-Gurion) as these Mizrachi Jews were considered a "rabble," a generation of the desert lacking a trace of Jewish or

Diaspora knew about this and turned a blind eye or helped in the cover-up is the subject of great debate.[1]

But an even more difficult question has to be asked. Is it any accident that both Sephardic and Mizrachi Jews are dark skinned? I hardly think so. It has taken an entire generation and more to begin to change this dynamic within the Israel Defense Forces (IDF) (nothing like being comrades in arms to build understanding and trust) and "intermarriage" between the groups (nothing like mixed, *chetzi-chetzi* [literally, "half and half"] grandchildren to build the love) serving as the great equalizers. Nevertheless, as anyone who has spent any time on the ground there will tell you, there is still a long way to go.

Many Jewish leaders like to point to the dramatic rescue and subsequent airlifts that brought the "lost Jews" of Ethiopia, *Beta Yisrael* as they call themselves, not *Falashas*, which has a negative connotation in their native language of Amharic, back to the Land of Israel as proof that we Jews are color blind.* Would that it was true. Would that Israel had learned from its earlier experience of discrimination to right the wrongs with this community of black brothers and sisters, cut off for centuries from any contact with us. But, sadly, it did not. Some would like to claim that it was the "backward nature" of their culture, the lack of education or modern skills that caused them to lag behind. Certainly that contributed. But is that why Depo-Provera, a hormonal injectable contraceptive, was regularly given to Ethiopian women about to immigrate to Israel? If those poor women asked the nurses or doctors what it was, they were told it was for their good health. The immediate result was a 20 percent decline in the birthrate for this "burdensome" population. Today, decades later, 65 percent of Ethiopian children live below the poverty line in the Land of Promise. In fact, according to the Taub Center, an independent, nonpartisan, socioeconomic research institute in Jerusalem, Ethiopian Israelis

---

human education. In fact, documents from the early days of the IDF indicate that Mizrachi recruits were often thought of as "retarded" and "incapable of being trained." In the last decade, many of these children have sought out and have been tearfully reunited with their biological parents and siblings.

*There were actually three airlifts—Operation Moses in 1984 (with the help of Sudan), which brought approximately eight thousand Jews; Operation Joshua, an American airlift of around five hundred Jews; and then Operation Solomon in 1991 that brought fourteen thousand.

(including those born in Israel and who served in the IDF) lag behind in test scores, academic degrees, and monthly salaries.[2]

Israel has broad antidiscrimination laws that prohibit discrimination by both government and nongovernment entities on the basis of race, religion, and political beliefs, and it prohibits incitement to racism. Israel is a state-party to the Convention on the Elimination of All Forms of Racial Discrimination, and is a signatory of the Convention against Discrimination in Education. All of this is good and looks good on paper. Nevertheless, Israel's president, Reuven Rivlin, announced to a meeting of academics in October 2014 that it is finally time for Israel to live up to its promise as a land of equality and time to cure the epidemic of racism. "Israeli society is sick, and it is our duty to treat this disease," Rivlin stated.[3] And this is to say nothing about widespread discrimination against Arab Israelis as well as Bedouins, many of whom also "happen" to be people of color.

But racial bias is not unique to Israel by any means. As of 2018, in a number of European nations we have seen the rise of right-wing parties with an anti-immigrant focus. It is no mere coincidence that the influx of immigrants in Europe are people of color, most often from parts of the world that Europeans themselves colonized, "stealing" their natural resources, establishing nations that combined ethnic and religious groups that had no business being together in the first place, and then walking out. The total disregard of these people's identities and needs while enriching their own nations, itself a racist act, is the root cause of much of the violence and unrest that we are witnessing today in the developing world. And now, instead of taking responsibility for the multiplicity of problems they caused, many Europeans wish to exclude and then blame their victims. As the church lady on *Saturday Night Live* used to say, "How convenient!"

This resurgence of populist right-wing parties in Europe has raised concerns in the American Jewish community, but, I would argue, for all the wrong reasons. Our almost exclusive and near total focus has been on the virulent anti-Semitism found among segments of the rising Muslim populations in Europe and protecting the Jewish communities and citizens there. While taking care of one's own is understandable, in effect, this has us siding with the racist right-wing parties, as has Israel's Benjamin Netanyahu, who has become quite cozy with Hungary's prime minister, Viktor Orban. Such an alliance is short sighted because these same hate groups have Jews on their list as well. Even though we have lived in Europe for more than a millennium, they still think of us as "usurpers" and impure, not real Europeans.*

The 2016 U.S. presidential election also exposed this chasm as Donald Trump would say, "Big League." "Make America Great Again" was felt by many as code for "make America white again." And the explosion of anti-immigrant (which is in actuality not so thinly veiled white supremacy), racist, and anti-Semitic acts around the nation that have been not-so-subtly encouraged and released by the president's election have many watchdog groups more than concerned. While the United States may very well be the greatest democracy in the world, the truth is that the nation was founded on white Protestant male privilege. The founding document of these United States, the much vaunted Constitution, did not recognize either women or black people as fully human, let alone as citizens. We might like to forget (Americans suffer from "short-term history-itis") that it took a civil war, Jim Crow laws, amendments to the Constitution, a civil rights movement, and then federal legislation over a period of almost two hundred years to right this wrong. The ongoing violence and police shootings especially of young black men would indicate that full equality is still a work in progress in our nation, with a strong, fully armed minority (now having crawled out of the ground, fully exposed) wishing to roll back the clock!

It is a matter of historical fact that immigration laws in the United States (even before quotas) favored whites as entry for Northern European and Germanic groups was far easier than all other peoples. As early as the nineteenth century, the United States attempted to exclude Chinese and other Asians from coming to this country. Northern Europeans were considered "superior." In the 1920s, as a reaction to the great influx of "certain peoples," quotas were put in place that favored immigration from Western Europe.† Need I remind you that in World War II it was

---

*There is a certain irony here that should not be lost on us. While these right-wing "nationalists" delegitimize Jews as non-Europeans, terrorist organizations like Hamas and Hezbollah want the "Zionists" to go back to Europe "where we belong!" I guess prejudice is never rooted in rational discourse.

† It was not until the Immigration and Nationality Act of 1965 that entry to the United States was dramatically opened to other groups, most of whom are people of color. Part of what we have seen in the 2016 presidential election in the United States, and in several European nations as well, is a fear of losing one's imagined place in the world as "better than them."

Japanese Americans who were forced into detention centers, not German Americans! Both nations, Germany and Japan, were our foreign enemies. Could there have been any reason other than race? As I write this, brown-skinned children who have done nothing wrong and have broken no laws, are being ripped out of the arms of their parents and placed in cages called "detention centers" all in the name of "securing our borders"! And nations with predominantly Muslim populations are on a list of countries banned for immigration, while calls for "quality immigrants" from countries like Norway dominate the president's rhetoric. This is not even thinly veiled racism. It is racism, pure and simple.

I recognize that I have gone a little far afield in this discussion, writing about European and American history. But I have done so in order to provide a context for understanding our own people's attitudes toward people of color. Context is determinative. Allow me please, then, to continue a bit longer. While our most common association with racism is acts of violence, abuse, or harassment (think white-hooded Klansmen), the truth is racism can be revealed through our attitudes. Actually, racism is the belief that solely because of skin color, all members of each race possess characteristics or abilities specific to that race so as to render one people inherently superior (or, alternatively, inferior) to another, and that a person's social and moral traits are predetermined by his inborn biological/racial characteristics. How strange! Biologists agree that the color of one's skin is, in scientific and genetic reality, a truly minor difference, determinant of practically nothing. In fact, geneticists agree that there are few genetic characteristics found in the population of, say, England that are not found in similar proportions in, say, Zaire or China. In other words, on a genetic level, we are all pretty much the same. Or another way of looking at it is this: the genetic differences within a so-called race, may, in fact, be greater than those between races! We are, each and every one of us, hybrids. There is no such thing as purity of race. Those differences that most deeply affect us in our dealings with each other are not to any significant degree biologically determined. And yet we act as if they are. (Sociologists Robert Kurzban, John Tooby, and Leda Cosmides note that race is one of the three characteristics most often used in brief descriptions of individuals. The other two are age and sex.)[4]

While there is clear ethnocentrism as far back as the Hebrew Bible (i.e., there are only two categories of people in the world—the

"Hebrews"/us, and the nations/all others/Gentiles/them), it was meant to keep the Israelites separate from the other peoples. Separation is a key category in the Hebrew Bible.* However, it has zero taint of being superior in some way. Even a cursory reading of the biblical text shows God's so-called chosen people to be incredibly flawed human beings. In fact, if we search the historical annals of the world, we find no evidence of racism prior to modernity.† In historian Dante Puzzo's famous assessment, "Racism . . . is a modern conception, for prior to the 16th century there was virtually nothing in the life and thought of the West that can be described as racist."⁵ What happened? What caused this rather large shift in human consciousness?

We like to believe that whites always thought of blacks as inferior and therefore enslaved millions of them. But the truth of the matter appears to be somewhat the opposite. When Portuguese sailors first explored Africa in the fifteenth and sixteenth centuries, they came upon empires and cities as advanced as their own, and according to their journals and letters, they considered Africans to be serious rivals. Later, the technological advances in Europe allowed the major powers to plunder the continent and colonize its inhabitants. This was the beginning of the shift.

Almost simultaneously, the European exploration of the New World began as a search for a shorter (and thereby cheaper) trade route to the much desired resources of the East. Remember, Columbus thought he landed in India, which is why we began to call the indigenous peoples of the Americas by the misnomer "Indians." While some of this exploration

---

*The Hebrew word *kadosh*, usually translated as "holy," comes from the root *kuf, dalet, shin*, which has the connotation of "separate." In the creation story, God separates light from darkness, land from sea, the Sabbath from the rest of the days of the week. The Land of Israel is *kadosh*, a separate place for a people who are to be separate from the nations in allegiance to a God who is also separate from the other gods. Kosher food is separate, and traditional dress is meant to separate, as is circumcision for males. The list can go on. Unfortunately, centuries of separation have led to a strain of xenophobia—fear and mistrust of "the other, the outsider"—for many Jews.

† If one looks at maps of Africa and/or the depiction of black people from that time forward, we see them drawn as animals (often apes) with exaggerated features, especially in contrast to whites in the same portraits. My son, whose university studies focused on colonialism, obtained one such early French map of Algeria. The French soldiers were dressed in beautiful uniforms, while the black people were mostly naked, in trees. In the past, Africans were accused of "selling their own" to assuage white guilt, fully ignoring that they were often warring tribes or nations. All of this (and more) was meant to dehumanize them so as to justify the barbaric treatment they received at the hands of their white captors and "owners."

might have had something to do with scientific curiosity, the dominating motivation was economic. Originally, when Europeans began in earnest to settle in the New World, they brought debtors and other petty criminal prisoners to the New World to work the land, promising freedom in exchange for their service. But as Europeans began to conquer the indigenous peoples through war and disease, the economic opportunities expanded, and this source of cheap labor was soon exhausted. Enter the slave trade with a seemingly unlimited supply of workers. But how does one square the inhumane treatment and the evils perpetrated on these poor, unsuspecting Africans with the so-called civilized enlightened attitudes promoting individual rights and human equality of Christian Europe? Simple. We are a superior race, and they are inferior. They are savages, a deficient species, beasts, the "white man's burden," and our task is to liberate them from their pagan beliefs and corrupt, immoral ways. In other words, racism (and all its subsequent pseudoscientific justifications like "Eugenics" and "polygenics") came into being to justify our enslavement of black people, not the other way around. (Hannah Arendt, in *The Origins of Totalitarianism*, corroborates this understanding, writing that racist ideology helped legitimize the imperialist conquest of foreign territories and the atrocities that [sometimes] accompanied them.)[6] And though they have been free and equal for more than a century and a half, the ugly belief, this scar on humanity, continues to persist.*

---

*Many parallels have been drawn between the biblical Exodus story and the African American civil rights movement. In fact, Reverend Martin Luther King Jr. often portrayed his people's struggle for equality as a modern-day Exodus, using the biblical tale to inspire his people to see beyond their struggles and to work together for the ultimate goal that was sure to come, just like it had for the ancient Israelites (Gary S. Selby, *Martin Luther King and the Rhetoric of Freedom* [Waco, TX: Baylor University Press, 2009]). The parallel was also embraced from the Jewish perspective, which led to the now famous Freedom *seder* and its accompanying Haggadah created by Rabbi Arthur Waskow. The first Freedom *seder* (third night of Passover, 1969) was celebrated in a black church in Washington, DC, attended by eight hundred people, half of them Jewish and half of them African Americans.

However, there is one major difference that ought not to be overlooked. Moses's confrontation with the pharaoh centered around his (God's) demand to "Let My people go!" Only outside of Egypt could we be a free people, worshipping our God. Though violated a thousand years later in Elephantine and Alexandria (great and powerful Jewish communities), the Torah forbids us to even go back to Egypt. Why? This has caused me to wonder for many years, had the Hebrew slaves been freed but never left Egypt, would we have developed into a distinct and proud independent nation? Or would the stigma of having once been slaves continued to diminish our potential and acceptance in that

I am not saying that all so-called white people or Ashkenazi Jews are racists. Far from it. We know for a fact that Jews were at the forefront of the civil rights movement in the United States, and the antiapartheid movement in South Africa; we were among the founders and early leaders of the National Association for the Advancement of Colored People. However, it would be more than naive to believe that as citizens of whatever nation we are not exposed to and influenced by all the cultural norms of our host society. After all, didn't Jewish landowners in the South own slaves just like their Christian neighbors while Jews in the north were strong supporters of the abolitionist movement? Most Jews in the United States are of European descent. Isn't it natural for us to declare (even if we refrain from saying it aloud) that we are not like "them"; we are like you, like all other Europeans? For centuries, Germans thought of themselves as superior to all others, an ingrained attitude that was exploited by Hitler and the Nazis. Well, didn't German Jews think they were superior to Eastern European Jews, an attitude that persisted long after they came to the Americas?*

---

nation? In other words, can the children, grandchildren, and now great-grandchildren of former slaveholders ever see the descendants of those slaves as full social equals?

In 1914, Marcus Garvey formed the Universal Negro Improvement Association (UNIA) with his revival of the mantra "Back to Africa" (also called, interestingly enough, "Black Zionism"). Though scorned by the black middle and professional classes, the UNIA became the largest mass movement in African American history. Garvey argued that African Americans' quest for social equality was a delusion. They were fated to be a permanent minority who could never assimilate because white Americans would never let them. Only in Africa was full emancipation possible, he believed. Though often attributed to him, the following words were actually written by Charles C. Seifert, to which I am certain Garvey would have said "Amen": "A people without the knowledge of their past history, origin, and culture is like a tree without roots" (Charles Seifert, *The Negro's or Ethiopian's Contribution to Art*, BCP Pamphlet [Baltimore, MD: Black Classic Press, 1986; originally published in 1938]). Ultimately, his movement failed while Dr. King's succeeded.

I merely raise the point to add to what needs to be a more open and difficult discussion on the dogged persistence of racism in our world, even though we know there is no good scientific or biological reason to hold such pejorative and destructive beliefs.

*I will never forget counseling with a congregant of mine in Milwaukee who unabashedly told me that he had more in common with his Gentile neighbors than "those Jews" who lived on the west side of town. His grandparents came from Germany; back then, the west side Jews were all from Poland and Russia, while those on the east side came from Germany. We absorbed many great cultural and intellectual gifts from our centuries of Jewish life in Germany. At the same time, it is no accident that we picked up on this "dis-ease" of the false belief at the core of racism that we are somehow superior. This same attitude kept many of my coreligionists believing they were safe from the Nazis, because, after all, they were German first and foremost and no harm could come to them. How tragic! Of my many Holocaust nightmares, one persistent image is that of the German

As citizens of nations with a history of racial discrimination, we are not immune from prejudice in all its forms. Is it merely an accident that Ashkenazi Jews who controlled Israel for most of its history discriminated against Mizrachi or dark-skinned Jews? Or that the first convert of mine who was denied citizenship in Israel on the basis of the Law of Return is a person of color? I know that we Jews like to think of ourselves as well-meaning liberals, and to a great extent, we are. But not all racism is obvious; often it is buried along with the belief that somehow one is superior. That hidden belief may have helped us survive millennia of prejudice and persecution. "We are better than them. They do not understand. They know not what they do. They are *bulvahns*" (from the Yiddish, literally an "ox" but referring to an undereducated person with no class, little sense, and low morals). That was then. Today the question is, "To what extent has the worldwide backlash against people of color affected, or should I say, 'infected' the Jewish community as well?"

I clearly remember Bobby Seale speaking on my college campus about the "white man" and agreeing with him. As a Jew in the United States, I never felt quite white. I was taught that there were only two places on earth—*aretz v'chootz'l'aretz* (the Land of Israel and outside the Land)—and that no matter how good life is in the Diaspora, it is still exile and we don't really belong. Then I realized that most of the African Americans in the crowd undoubtedly thought he was also talking about me as well. To the Ku Klux Klan, we were not white like them; and to the black power movement, we were "whitey"! What a shock to my system! Nowadays, when filling out forms, I check "other" when it comes to race or ethnicity. Nevertheless, despite our liberal record, I think we would be fooling ourselves if we did not admit to a kind of benign racism that affects our attitude toward people of color as somehow "not quite like us." After all, when my parents referred to them as *schwartzes*, they did not mean "black people." Just like *goy* did not mean "member of another nation." These were pejorative terms, indicative of a kind of felt superiority. While I fully understand how an oppressed minority might want to cultivate a feeling of "being better than them" as a way to inoculate themselves from the prejudice aimed against them, I cannot condone it. None of us should.

Jew in line to the concentration camps with "Jews of the East" wondering what he is doing there, that there must be some mistake. That he is not like "them." Tragedy indeed!

I grew up in New York City and did not even know there was a community of black Jews living in Brooklyn, nor did I ever even hear of the rich Sephardic history of the American Jewish community, let alone the rest of the world. It was as if they never existed, even though for hundreds of years the only Jews in America were of Sephardic descent, and for most of Jewish history, Judaism was kept alive by the Jews of North Africa and the Middle East. It is as if we expunged them from our collective memory, replacing them with Tevye and Golda.* And though the story of how the Danish king and his entire population wore the yellow star rather than allow the Nazis to deport his Jewish population to the gas chambers, thus saving the five thousand or so Danish Jews, was burnished into my consciousness, until a recent trip to his country, I never learned that the king of Morocco did the same exact thing, saving a quarter of a million of my people! I wonder why.

The term "aversive racism" was coined by Joel Kovel to describe a form of implicit racism in which a person's unconscious negative evaluations of racial or ethnic minorities are realized by a persistent avoidance of interaction with other racial and ethnic groups.[7] As opposed to traditional overt racism, which is characterized by obvious hatred for and explicit discrimination against minorities, aversive racism is characterized by more complex, ambivalent expressions and attitudes. People who think and/or behave in an aversively racial way may profess egalitarian beliefs, while denying their racially motivated behavior; nevertheless, they often change their behavior when dealing with a member of another race.

I never knew a member of the Ku Klux Klan. My people were not invited to join. Yet I clearly remember asking my mom if it was okay for me to invite my new fifth-grade friend Clyde home after school one day. "Of course!" she replied. A few days later, after a fun afternoon and Clyde went home, my mother asked, "Why didn't you tell me Clyde was a *schwartze*?" It had never occurred to me that it mattered to her, and it certainly did not matter to me. I was brought up to treat all people with

---

*I was once told of an experiment conducted in Israeli public schools that asked elementary students of all backgrounds and ethnicities to draw a Jew; however, in all honesty, I have no proof that it was actually carried out. The vast majority of them drew a picture of an Ashkenazi Hasid, even though none of the students were Orthodox. This image of us as white and European has obviously been ingrained into the consciousness of our own people, let alone the rest of the world. And since it sits in defiance of historical reality, sadly, it is safe to say that the very core of this belief is racist in nature.

respect. I loved Viry, the black woman who cleaned our apartment when I was a child. At the same time, I do recall my mother referring to her as "my colored girl." That's "aversive racism." We are all exposed to it.

Fast forward forty plus years, I visited my youngest son at college. He was living off campus with two new roommates whom I would be meeting for the first time. I walked into his house and was greeted by two young women, one of whom was black. Ezra never said anything to me about the identity of his roommates. And yet, after introductions were made, the incident with Clyde and my mother popped into my head. I heard myself asking, "Why didn't you tell me your roommates were female and black?" But, fortunately, I did not. Still, I get that my even thinking it is a subtle form of racism. As mayor of New Orleans Mitch Landrieu recently said in defending his decision to remove Civil War statues from his city, "We all take our own journey when it comes to race."[8]

In my work in Latin America, I have seen this firsthand. With few exceptions, most of the Jewish communities in Latin America today are dominated by Ashkenazi Jews who fled Europe prior, during, and immediately after the Holocaust. Most of them have been enormously successful. They live in guarded mansions, drive expensive cars, and enjoy all the privileges of the upper class. And without exception, they have been dismissive of the emerging Jewish communities claiming historic connection to the *b'nai anusim* (the crypto Sephardic Jews of Spain and Portugal who survived the Inquisition and kept their Jewish connection, their birthright, a secret). I know of too many incidents in which people of color seeking entry into the community's synagogues are sent away and not even allowed to worship there. They are dismissed without reason, to be "discarded like so much trash."

Now I realize some of their rejection has to do with classism, a dominant feature of Latin American societies. Like members of exclusive country clubs, they do not wish to associate with "them," those people of lower class. Some of it, I am certain, is based on protecting their hard-won status and privilege. But is it any accident that almost all of those seeking to return to Judaism are people of color? Mixed race? Assimilated DNA? The established community argues that these people are insincere, or not "really Jewish," or that they are really "*messiancos*" (what we call in the United States "Jews for Jesus") with a secret agenda to convert us to Christianity. But the truth is these emerging Jews are way more observant of Jewish tradition than our Ashkenazi brothers and sisters who sit in judgment of them. This is not an argument over observance of Jewish law. Very few of the Ashkenazi Jews are *shomer Shabbat* (Sabbath observers), pray regularly, keep kosher, wear *tzitzit* (fringes), or cover their heads. For all intents and purposes, their lives and lifestyles are not very different from their Christian neighbors. The irony is that many of the men have second wives (and/or mistresses) who are Latina and often women of color. I am reminded that slave owners in the United States often had sexual relations with their black slaves, yet their racism continued unabated. Can it be that our Jewish brothers and sisters in Latin America have absorbed this racism from their host countries? After all, during the Spanish colonial period, the Spaniards developed a complex caste system based on race, which was used for social control and which also determined a person's importance in society. While many Latin American countries have long since rendered the system officially illegal, prejudice based on degrees of perceived racial distance from European ancestry (combined with one's socioeconomic status) remains an echo of the racist past. No doubt this is a factor in the almost complete lack of acceptance, if not outright rejection, of the return of the *b'nai anusim* throughout the Latin Americas.

Our Torah teaches us that a "mixed multitude" went out from Egypt. Though it does not explain what that meant, given our history and the centuries we spent living there, I am certain they were of mixed races, various ethnicities, multiple cultures, and probably held a multiplicity of religious ideas. There is even speculation that Moses himself might have been black.* Though they were "stiff necked" and rebellious, somehow they were able to unite and become one people. The people who wish to return to Judaism today do not look like my *bubbe* (grandmother) and *zayde* (grandfather). To embrace them would literally change the face of the Jewish people. Either this poses a threat or an opportunity. I fully believe it is the latter, a veritable rainbow of Jewish people! For our chil-

---

*The argument goes that since the Egyptian pharaoh at the time was a descendant of Ham (the progenitor of the black race) who adopted him as "his own son," he must have been black as well. This may have merit as in the only potentially race-related passage in the Torah, Numbers 12:1, Aaron and Miriam are bad-mouthing their brother Moses for having married a "Cushite woman." If, in fact, Cush was a land of dark-skinned people, then this might have been a racial slur. What happened next? Miriam is stricken with a leprosy-like condition as punishment for what she said. In Modern Hebrew, to call someone a *"cushi"* is akin to using the "n" word in English.

dren, this is already pro forma. They are truly color-blind when it comes to race; they live in an inclusive world. And the wealth of commercials on television that regularly feature racially mixed couples and families are a clear indication that the contemporary culture accepts it as well. It is past time for Jewish leadership to get with this program. Racial diversity—in fact, all diversity—is a strength and a validation of the Jewish value that we are all created in the image of God.

And yet, what has been the response of the established Jewish community either in Israel or the United States? What efforts and what resources are being expended to save and rescue these communities? What resources are being used to help educate and deepen their Jewish connections? Which seminaries are training rabbinic students, cantors, and educators to spend an internship strengthening these communities? Which *shalichim* (outreach emissaries) from Israel are being trained and sent to connect them to our Homeland? What Jewish Community Centers are being built? Which Jewish Federations are allocating some of their overseas funds to help these Jews? What efforts are being made by the Joint Distribution Committee on the ground or the American Jewish Committee in the political sphere? How is the Jewish Agency encouraging their travel or *alliyah* to Israel? I will save you the time in researching responses to these questions. Nada. Nothing. *Shum d'var*. It is one of the greatest opportunities to expand the reach and depth of the Jewish community that ever existed, and most Jews literally know nothing about it. Again, I ask, is it any coincidence that these are Jews of color?*

In his TED Talk, "Fixing Racism," Dr. Gurdeep Parhar states that we need to "recognize that we all have subconscious bias, bring it to the forefront, and deal with it."[9] We all stereotype. Our brains automatically put things into neat categories. It is just what we humans do. And yet, people aren't born with racist ideas or attitudes; it is taught and learned. What Dr. Parhar, himself a victim of prejudice, suggests is that this, in and of itself, is not the problem. The problem is we deny it. I saw this

---

*Though I explore this topic more fully in the chapter titled "Israel: Ingathering or Impediment?," the Knesset recently voted to *not* recognize the Abayudaya community of Jews in Uganda. Though small in number today, estimates range into the millions of Africans who may have a genetic connection dating back millennia. Happily, both the Conservative and Reform movements have accepted these brothers and sisters. Their rabbi, Gershom Sizomu, was educated at the Jewish Theological Seminary in New York. Ironically, the Abayudaya were persecuted under the reign of Idi Amin for their religious beliefs.

played out in the gubernatorial election in Florida this past year (2018). The Republican candidate, Ron Desantis, running against an African American, Andrew Gillum, used the term "monkey around," which offended the black community. He denied it had any racial overtones. One black woman challenged him, saying, "You do not get to tell us what is offensive; we decide what offends us, not the other way around." I loved that she stood up in that way!

After decades of denial, it is essential that the Jewish community own its own history of racism and begin to take responsibility for it. It is in this way, and this way only, that we can have open and honest dialogue so that we can make both the internal as well as external changes that are necessary to alter the future. Racism—the diminishment of an entire group of people and the destruction of human possibility—diminishes us all. If we are truly going to move "beyond survival," it cannot come at the expense of any other individual or group. The thriving of the Jewish people means the thriving of all people, everywhere. Though referred to as one, we Jews have never been a race. What a disgrace, at this moment in our people's history, should we seek to become one now.

Part II

OPPORTUNITIES

Who Is a Jew?

$\mathscr{I}$n 2010, a friend took me to see Zachary Balber's powerful photographic exhibit in Miami's Wynwood art district. The collection was called *Tamim* (Hebrew for "pure"), and it consisted of larger-than-life photographs of Jews whose bodies were either disfigured in some way or covered with tattoos. The juxtaposition of the title with the images before my eyes was not lost on me. According to Jewish law, Jews are forbidden to scar their bodies in any way. "You shall not make gashes in your flesh for the dead, or incise any marks on yourselves: I am the Lord" (Lev. 19:28). Nor could a priest have any physical blemish (Lev. 21:18–20). As children, we were told if you did so, you would not be able to be buried in a Jewish cemetery. Though this is untrue, a real *bubbe meisa* (grandma story) if ever there was one, it still lives in the popular imagination as one of those boundary issues. I cannot tell you how many times a parent dragged their young teenage child to my study saying something like, "Rabbi, tell her if she gets a tattoo she won't get buried in a Jewish cemetery. Tell her!" And then I have to deliver the "bad" news to the unfortunate parent—"though prohibited by Jewish law, no one will keep you out of a Jewish cemetery when the time comes, many, many years from now!" Sorry, Mom. Sorry, Dad.

During the Holocaust, the Nazis purposely tattooed numbers on the arms of Jews in violation of this biblical precept to further humiliate our people. Once upon a time, if a Jew chose to be tattooed, he probably hid it from most people's view. But now, less than a century after the Nazis' heinous dehumanization of our people, Jews are consciously choosing this prohibited act without any ambivalence, even proudly displaying Jewish symbols, the numbers that were on their grandparents' arms, as well as Hebrew words, quotes from sacred texts, even God's unpronounceable name YHVH (*yud*, *hey*, *vav*, *hey*) as part of their body art. My last visit to the Tel Aviv beach was no less than an eye opener. There were more tattoos than people! And it is not just our own people doing this. I cannot tell you how many times I have seen Jewish symbols and/or Hebrew words tattooed on the bodies of people of other faiths.* What is going on here?

My parents were Jewish. I don't mean they were born Jews, even though they were. Their entire identity, the people with whom they associated, the neighborhoods in which they lived, their worldview (which could be summed up as "us versus them"), the causes with which they identified—there was not a single element of their lives that were not infused with *yiddishkeit* (though not literally translatable, I would say *yiddishkeit* is a worldview that is infused with Jewish life and culture—seeing the world through Jewish eyes). My parents were not religious people, though my father, with me in tow, did make the annual pilgrimage to the synagogue on the High Holy Days, and when the roll call for donations took place, stood up proudly pledging more money than we could afford. Of course, we gathered at my *bubbe* and grandpa's house each Passover, while the adults talked among themselves and my grandfather sped read the entire *haggadah* with me dutifully sitting at his side. But the most religious rite bar none that we carried on, without failure, with complete fidelity, along with many of our Jewish neighbors, was Sunday night dinner at the local Chinese restaurant where we could eat any manner of *traife* (unkosher food) so long as we did not order any dish with the word "pork" in it. Spare ribs, won tons, and egg rolls were all fine. Funny but true.

Once upon a time, and not so very long ago, Jews all over the world lived together in sequestered communities. Whether this was imposed upon us from the outside (like the gated ghettos and secluded *shtetls* of Europe or the *melahs* in the Muslim world) or those chosen by our-

---

*I was at my chiropractor one day when I saw this woman sitting across from me, wearing a big crucifix and sporting a rather large *magen David* tattoo on the inside of her forearm. So I asked her, "I see you with both a crucifix and a Jewish star. I am a rabbi and am curious. What is your religious identity if you don't mind my asking?"

"Not at all," she replied. "I am a Christian. When I went to Israel with my church last year, I fell in love with the Land and the people, so I got this tattoo to show my solidarity. I can't wait to go back."

"And where did you get the perfect tat?"

"Oh! In Tel Aviv," she replied, as if that was the most natural thing in the world.

selves—like the Jewish communities that dotted the worldwide landscape (Shaker Heights in Cleveland; Colfax Avenue in Denver; Fairfax in Los Angeles; Skokie in Chicago; Lower East Side in New York; West End in London; Le Marais in Paris; etc.) —Jews lived together, worked side by side, socialized with and married other Jews. There was no doubt about who was a Jew, and if anyone tried to "pass" for a Gentile, the outside world was often quick to remind us that we did not belong. Internally, by and large, we agreed with Jewish law that anyone born of a Jewish mother or an individual who converted to Judaism was a Jew. Now all of that began to change with the advent of the so-called Enlightenment in Western Europe toward the end of the eighteenth century. The change was accelerated in the United States. What has happened in the course of the last two hundred years?

When Napoleon began to tear down the ghetto walls, beginning in Germany, not France, Jews left in droves. They embraced the opportunity to live anywhere, to attend the university, to work at any profession, to join the culture of their new national identity. And to gain full acceptance, many of these Jews began to convert to Christianity. To stem that tide, Reform Judaism was established (by a lay person, Israel Jacobson—the rabbis were slow to catch on) so that Jews could be both Germans/French/British *and* Jews. It was a new reality, as prior to this time Jews were not considered citizens of their native lands. And once begun in Western Europe, like many great ideas, over the course of the next century, it would gradually but definitively spread to the New World and Eastern Europe as well.*

Of course, this change did not happen overnight. Jews continued to face discrimination, quotas, anti-Semitism, and the like. In part, Jewish success in all the walks of life that became available to us led to the horrors of the Holocaust as Hitler capitalized on the age-old false fear of the Jew (as the foreign, not-to-be-trusted outsider) taking over. However, even in the face of genocide, we ultimately found full acceptance. Today nothing is denied our children. They have complete and full access in education,

---

*For the entirety of the Middle Ages, Jews had special status in whatever place they lived. At times, this status was protected by the local authority or leader, but at other times, this status was revoked or the Jews were banished altogether. Many of these court letters have been preserved and can be read in an excellent book, *The Jew in the Medieval World*, by Jacob Rader Marcus.

profession, choice of the friends with whom they associate, and place of residence. And with the exception of a small number of Orthodox Jews who continue to live in self-imposed neighborhoods (like Eastern Parkway and Williamsburg in Brooklyn; Muncie, New York; Antwerp, Belgium; Meah Shearim, Jerusalem, among others) the vast majority of Jews live no differently than our neighbors of different faiths or no faith. In fact, when I ask a Jewish adult, "If I followed you around for a few days, how would I know from your behavior that you are Jewish?" the vast majority are at a loss to answer the question. For the most part, even when committed to Jewish continuity, Jews look, believe, dress, eat, speak, and behave like most of their fellow countrymen. And while their homes might have a *mezuzah* (marker of a Jewish home) on the doorpost, once inside, the furnishings and art look a lot like what is found in the homes of their neighbors of different faiths.

In short, the number one assumption of more than two thousand years of Jewish life in the Diaspora—that Jewish identity is automatic and can be assumed—is no longer operative. I cannot emphasize enough just how radical this is. Previous generations had no choice; their lives were intimately entwined with those of other Jews, members of the tribe. Whether they were personally religious or whether they believed in the major tenets of Judaism, still they "had to be" Jews. Yes, they could always convert to another faith and were, at times, pressured to do so. But doing that meant a complete break with everything and everyone they knew. Their families and the entire community "sat *shivah*" for them. For all intents and purposes, they were as good as dead. Facing such isolation that bounded on "excommunication" (*cherem* in Hebrew), very few chose that path, especially in modern America. Today, however, for the vast majority of us, for multiple reasons, that threat no longer exists.

And there is another key factor in today's world that cannot be overlooked. In all societies of the past, admission and identity were confirmed by the group onto the individual. Illegal immigration aside, in nations, one does not declare oneself a citizen; folks have to apply for citizenship and go through a prescribed path. Similarly, in Judaism, the infant male child is brought to the community for acceptance into the Jewish people. Unless trained to do so themselves, the parents present their eight-day-old son to the one acting as *mohel* to perform the ancient rite of circumcision, which serves as his physical ticket of admission. It is through this rite with the accompanying blessings that identity is confirmed and then his name is announced and the community affirms the parents' action, thereby welcoming this newest member into the community.

Until recently, girl babies were welcomed unceremoniously. Literally. Her father would come to a synagogue on the Shabbat morning after she was born and be given an *alliyah* to the Torah, after which a *mi sheberach* (healing prayer) was said for her and her mother. During this prayer, the baby's name would be announced for the first time in public, thereby automatically welcoming her into the community. In an effort to be egalitarian, recognizing female status as separate from her father, today, girl babies are presented to the community with what has come to be called a "*brit bat,*" a covenant of a daughter, with creative rituals such as the lighting of two candles by the female elders of the family (symbolizing the candles she will hopefully one day light); or the wrapping of the baby in a *tallit* (prayer shawl) representing the feminine presence of the Divine *Shechinah*; or the washing of the baby's feet, symbolizing the *mikveh* (ritual bath or immersion in water), just to name a few.

In other words, for millennia (with the exception of voluntary adult conversion), the path to becoming a Jew had nothing to do with the advice or consent of the individual. It was the community that conferred identity on a baby who obviously had no say in the matter. And even in cases in which an adult converted to Judaism, the rituals performed mimicked that of a child born to Jewish parents—*mikveh* (symbolic of the womb); circumcision or *hatafaht dahm* (the drop of blood taken from the glans of the penis for those already circumcised); and the announcement of the name at the *bet din* (the rabbinic court representing the community) or at a communal worship service when the one who has chosen Judaism is called up for an *alliyah* to the Torah. And when children of converts also convert, they are treated like the children of born Jews—that is, their parents enter them into the covenant with the consent of the *bet din*. In other words, traditionally, the group admits and confers identity on the individual; we have been doing so for thousands of years and so did most cultures and religious faiths.

Now while these rituals continue to exist, and we act as if nothing has changed, the mind-set of our culture is 180 degrees opposite. And the very notion of identity has changed along with it. As stated earlier, in a premodern time, identity was conferred by the group onto the individual.

If you wanted in, you had to abide by the entry rules. Every group had them, and you messed with them at your peril. (Think about the Reform movement's passage of Patrilineal Descent as an example in which they added "born of a Jewish mother *or* father." More on that later.) Today, in what is being called the "postmodern period," there is weaker commitment to group identity throughout the world.* As a result, identity today is individual and self-selected. I say who I am; no one gets to decide for me. And more and more, who I say I am is very complicated and nuanced and easily multiple.

The point is this: personal identity today is just that—it's personal. It is also extremely meaningful to the individual. (Just look at all of the DNA testing for one's ancestry being advertised on television these days. According to *MIT Technology Review*, more than twelve million people had their DNA tested in 2017. The magazine estimates that one out of every twenty Americans has now participated in some kind of genetic testing. It is a multibillion-dollar industry!)[1] And, this is important for the Jewish community to hear—in addition, identity is fractional and multi-dimensional. That is to say, people are no longer seeing themselves as one thing or another. Identity today means a number of things to people. We all belong to a variety of groups that help define us. One can be Jewish and Hispanic with ancestors from Spain and Denmark, as well as a scientist and a practitioner of Yoga and . . . you get the picture. And what makes it even more challenging—now hear this—is that (with the exception of some rabbis) no one believes anyone else has the right to decide. We can continue to pretend and act as if we have the authority to make these decisions for others; they will go about their business largely ignoring, at best, even becoming hostile, at worst, to the dictates and claims of the larger group. In today's world, like it or not, each individual chooses or decides who she or he is, not the group.

As mentioned previously, back in March 1983 the Central Conference of American Rabbis, the Reform movement's umbrella organization of rabbis, influenced by the sociological reality of growing intermarriage, the desire to be fully egalitarian, and shifting identity patterns, passed the very controversial and largely misunderstood Patrilineal Descent Ruling. In some ways, this ruling attempted to be more inclusive and, in other

---

*In the Jewish community, this shows up in the divide between "covenantal Jews" versus "tribal Jews," the former being personal and the latter being group.

ways, stricter or more narrow. Basically, the ruling stated that anyone born of a Jewish mother or father who demonstrates timely acts of Jewish identity (like *brit milah* [ritual circumcision], *Bar* or *Bat Mitzvah* [formal Jewish education], etc.) shall be considered Jewish. In other words, the Reform movement determined that DNA counts, but only so much. The choices we make are also important. Identity is both given and chosen. The other movements rejected the decision relying on the traditional *halachic* standard that only one born of a Jewish mother or converted is considered a Jew, warning that such a stance would, in effect, create two separate Jewish peoples and that we would be unable to marry one another's children. That remains a possibility. Ultimately, the Reconstructionist movement also adapted Patrilineal Descent as determinative of Jewish status.*

In my first pulpit, I was approached by a young woman who wanted to be part of our congregation. In sharing her story, she reported that her mother was Jewish, her father was Presbyterian, and she was raised as a nominal Christian, with practically no formal Jewish education or involvement. She was a single mother of a young boy, and they were searching for a spiritual home. Judaism was calling to her. I was quite moved by her story. Nevertheless, I suggested that she go through a formal conversion, together with her son, as a way of demarcating this great transition and rite of passage in their lives. She was very quiet for a couple of minutes and then replied, "But the Chabad rabbi said we are both Jews." I really felt for her and I tried to explain as lovingly as I could that my suggestion of a conversion process was for her and her son's benefit, but she could not hear me. I wished her well as she declared they would be joining Chabad. Around eight months later, she came to see me again. It wasn't working for them. They did not "feel" Jewish even though they were always included in the activities of the synagogue. We decided to do *mikveh* for both of them and *hatafaht dam* for her son combined with

---

*It seems clear that matrilineal descent was, in its time, a sociological adaptation as well. In the Torah, the children of Jacob as well as Joseph, born to non-Jewish mothers, were considered Jews. Of course, the medieval rabbis comment that these women converted to Judaism, but there is absolutely no biblical evidence to support that story. To this day, we bless our sons in the names of Ephraim and Menasseh, Joseph's "half-Jewish" sons. It appears that the rabbis changed the descent rule in response to the large number of Jewish women who were raped and became pregnant when Jewish communities were attacked and many males slaughtered. As an act of compassion, the rabbis considered these children Jewish, which meant the community would help support them. In order to make the biblical children "kosher," they subsequently made up the conversion story of these mothers.

a communal welcome and *bet din*. Years later we celebrated her son becoming a *Bar Mitzvah* and she joining our board of directors. For me, this was a corroboration of what I think we all know today—identity is complex and highly personal, impacted primarily by the choices we make and the lives we live.

We already know that there are hundreds of thousands of Jews of Patrilineal Descent, perhaps more who no longer consider themselves Jews because of the rejection and hostility they have faced from segments of the Jewish world that tell them, "You know you are not really Jewish!" when they share that they were born to a mother who was not Jewish and who did not convert to Judaism. We are only talking here about those individuals whose father is Jewish, who were raised as Jews, who celebrated becoming a *Bar/Bat Mitzvah*, who were active in their Temple's Youth Group, who traveled to Israel, who were leaders at their college Hillel or Jewish fraternity/sorority. When asked what religion they are, they immediately and proudly responded, "I'm Jewish!" Yet, often by Jews who are minimally involved themselves, they were wounded by the response, "No, you're not!" I know. Too many times they have called me in tears from their college campuses.

In addition, there are an untold number of people who made the often difficult decision to convert to Judaism under the auspices of a Reform, Conservative, Reconstructionist, or a Jewish Renewal rabbi. Often, this meant hurting the feelings and disturbing relationships within their birth families. Nevertheless, they did so and continue to live meaningful Jewish lives. There is not a synagogue or Jewish organization in the world today that hasn't benefited from the energy and commitment of these individuals who freely chose and embraced Judaism. Yet, there are some in the ultra-Orthodox community who would like to invalidate their journey, exclude them from our people, or insist they must be "re-converted." There even exists a so-called blacklist of rabbis, some of whom are modern Orthodox, whose conversions are no longer being accepted in Israel. How incredibly hurtful, even wounding, for these true members of our communal family!

The implications of all this are enormous and one of the reasons that the United Jewish Communities who had partnered with the Jewish Federation system stopped doing the North American Jewish Population Survey. The last one was in the year 2000. It was fraught with so much difficulty and disagreement because, within a broad range of criteria, the individuals questioned were allowed to say whether they were Jewish or not. For example, a person born of a Jewish father, raised as a Jew, who celebrated his *Bar Mitzvah* and today belongs to a synagogue with his children who are also being raised as Jews, responded in the affirmative; while a woman, born of a Jewish mother, who today attends a Buddhist Temple responded in the negative. Messianic Jews who were called also responded in the affirmative. Examples abound. There was no consensus in the Jewish world over who to count as Jewish, which is why today we say that there are between 5.7 and 6.8 million, with some estimates as high as 7.1 million Jews in the United States! That's an enormous differential. To avoid the aggravation and controversy, the Jewish Federations of North America gratefully handed over the census task to the Pew Foundation, which continues to do a good job with it. I guess since they are Gentiles, we can at least trust that their motives are pure as they have no "skin in the game"! There is a kind of painful irony in this for me. As a group, we are, in the twenty-first century, unable to decide for ourselves who is a member of our own community.

But the question of "Who is a Jew?" does not revolve solely around religious identity. DNA screenings are revealing that there are very few, if any "pure breeds" in the human family. While we *Homo sapiens* may have begun with a small genetic sampling, each of us has become an admixture of many different strands. It is not uncommon for someone to say today, "I am one-sixteenth this, and one-eighth that, one-thirty-second . . ." We have all seen the commercials with the pie chart. You get the picture. The news of one's mixed genetic identity is life transforming. What is true of our ancestry is also true of our sexuality and certainly true of the groups (plural) with whom we associate. Unlike my parents' generation, today we take part in multiple communities, both professional and personal, that help define us.

The identity question has gotten pretty dicey in Israel. The Law of Return stipulates that any individual who has at least one Jewish grandparent or has converted in a recognized rabbinic court outside the State of Israel may apply for instantaneous citizenship. The Law of Return does not, however, provide for such a citizen's automatic recognition as Jewish by the Israeli Chief Rabbinate. Sounds crazy, right? Currently, it is estimated that some four hundred thousand Israelis (mostly from Russia and Ukraine) are officially listed as having "no religion."[2] Such "no-man's land" status means they cannot get married in Israel or even be buried in a Jewish cemetery. Most are willing to go along with the demand to convert to Judaism, but the officially recognized rabbinic courts there (all ultra-Orthodox) only handle about two thousand conversions a year. It is bitterly ironic that in the State of Israel, even when one is living there, it is a hurdle to be considered Jewish! And the longer this goes on, the greater the chance is that we will lose their children and grandchildren as members of the worldwide Jewish people.

Believe it or not, it gets even more complicated. All over the world today we are witnessing emerging Jewish communities who claim descent from the time of the Bible and are declaring themselves to be Jewish, often citing ancient connections to Israel. Some say they are the children of Menelik, the son of the Queen of Sheba (1 Kings 10) who left Jerusalem and traveled to Africa after he was passed over to succeed his father Solomon on the throne. Others claim descent to the so-called lost tribes who were dispersed during the first exile in the seventh century BCE. And still others have embraced Judaism in the last century. Whether one believes these legends, those claiming Jewish identity do hold them as sacred. Many are living ostensibly observant Jewish lives (certainly more observant than my parents were); have few, if any learned local authorities; and are *not* necessarily seeking the Jewish establishment's seal of approval. An isolated instance of this here and there could easily be dismissed or written off. However, in Africa alone their numbers could total into the millions. The same is true of the *b'nai anusim* in North, Central, and South America, as well as in parts of Europe. Today many seek acceptance through conversion. But what if they merely begin to assert Jewish identity and live Jewish lives, claiming their birthright that was stolen from them some five hundred years ago? There is no denying that they are there; history corroborates that. We are fast reaching the point where "they" (i.e., the emerging Jewish communities) might outnumber those of us who are considered the in-group, with estimates ranging from fifteen to twenty-five million people worldwide. Ignoring the reality, which seems to be the current stance of the established Jewish community, will not make it go away.

And finally, though much more controversial, we have numerous communities, organizations, and individuals spread throughout the world who have accepted Jesus as their Messiah. While this movement may have begun as a pernicious subterfuge to convert Jews to Christianity, it no longer really operates that way. Rather, we find these "synagogues" and their "rabbis" praying and behaving like any other Jewish community with the addition of a theology that we have defined as over the line and unacceptable—that is, that the much awaited and longed for *Mashiach* (Messiah) has not yet come to redeem us. Whether it was Jesus of Nazareth, or any of the others who laid claim to being the Messiah, over the last two millennia the Jewish community as a whole, rejected those claims.* Yet those inside those communities self-define as Jews, are supportive of Israel, see themselves as allies to the Jewish world, and, more and more, seek to be a part of mainstream Jewish organizations (often keeping their beliefs to themselves for fear of being ostracized). After all, if it is okay to be a secular atheist, denying any authority to the Torah or Jewish law, and still be considered Jewish, why is it not okay to be an observant Jew who happens to accept that the Messiah has already been here and will one day return to clean up all of our collective mess? We say that we are a religion that values behavior/deed over belief/creed. Since when has a particular belief (other than one God, which, after all, has been "on the books" for quite some time) been determinant of Jewish identity? By the way, if the proverbial line in the sand is Judaism's belief that the Messiah has not yet come, why is Chabad, which believes that their Rebbe Menachem Schneerson (who died in 1994) is the *Mashiach*, still considered inside the line? Now I am not suggesting they be cast out of our people; rather, as a community, we seem to want to have it both ways on this issue. Clearly, this is a truly uncomfortable conversation that the Jewish community does not want to have!

Recently, at a workshop I helped facilitate, I met Zipporah, a black Evangelical pastor who was admiring my *tallit*. I asked her about her name, and she proudly told me that each of her siblings, and now her own children, have Hebrew biblical names to honor their Jewish roots. She herself wears a *tallit* when she leads worship at her church. So many

---

*For an excellent discussion of the history of this rather complex theological debate, I recommend Gershom Scholem's *The Messianic Idea in Judaism and Other Essays on Jewish Spirituality* (New York: Schocken Books, 1971). Though not easy to read, in it he details the rich and interesting history of this concept, highlighting some of the colorful characters who were followed as the Messiah, including Sabbatai Zevi and Jacob Frank.

times I have met like-minded Christians who display zero ambivalence about embracing core elements of Judaism in their expression of their Christian faith. My friend, Father Gerry, who calls me his rabbi, is always quick to remind me that Jesus was a good Jew. Now I am not saying that these untold numbers of Christians should be included in the next Jewish census. After all, I have argued in this chapter that, in today's reality, identity is self-determined. But what if, in the imaginary checklist of identity, millions of Christians have the option of "part-Jewish"? What would the organized Jewish community do then? Can we handle the fact that instead of seeing themselves as supersessionists (i.e., replaced Judaism) many in today's Christian world want to join us?

In addition to that, there are now people all over the world who have no intention of being Jewish but who are at the same time adopting and including Jewish practices and principles into their lives—studying *Kabbalah*, getting married under a *chuppah* (wedding canopy) and breaking a glass at their weddings, having thirteen-year-old coming-of-age celebrations, spending quality time in Israel, creating and participating in an annual *seder*—just to name a few. The medical assistant at my chiropractor's office told me her sister and her brother-in-law (neither of them Jewish) were married by a Kabbalistic rabbi. The family loved it! At the Jewish Home in Florida, I heard two African American, crucifix-wearing aides excitedly describe to a new resident who is a Christian how they love their communal Shabbat celebration. In Senegal, there is a group of Muslims who call themselves "Bani Israel." They are proud Muslims who are also proud of their Jewish heritage and supportive of the State of Israel. Several words in their language of Wolof have Hebrew origin. Who knows how many other groups like this will be emerging in the coming decades? In other words, throughout the world, people today are comfortable with including and incorporating some aspects of Judaism into their lives. Once upon a time, we were a despised faith, a "guttural" religion; now we are sought out, respected, and honored. It seems to me that we need to find a way to embrace our newfound friends.

But beyond the numbers a more significant issue arises. Who has the right to tell them they are not Jews? In the absence of a single authority (for better or worse, we have no pope), who will decide? In the history of the Jewish people, these kinds of rifts—Sadducees-Samaritans, Rabbinites-Kararites, and Hasidim-Mitnagdim, for example—occurred with each group declaring that the other was not really Jewish, pro-nouncing a ban of *cherem* upon one another. In some instances, whole groups were lost and disappeared. That could have happened with the Ethiopian Jews as well, the *Beta Yisrael*, but fortunately it did not. But, and here is the key point, in each of those cases *the authority to determine identity was not challenged*, only the one who was doing the determining. That is *not* today's reality. Presently, no one has a monolith on Jewish authority. Even in Israel, where the government has ceded political power to the ultra-Orthodox rabbinate, the majority of the population is indifferent at best, hostile at worst. Today, more and more, we are self-authorized. I see no getting around that. And unless we all get on that same page, we may yet find ourselves with multiple Jewish peoples. The implications for that, especially at this moment in time, I think we could all agree, would be disastrous.

On the other hand, if we embrace what is de facto the reality, we have an opportunity to greatly increase both the diversity and numbers of the Jewish people. And both of those will greatly increase our strength and our ability to thrive. I fully understand that the number one fear in this regard is the dilution of Judaism. In other words, if we adopt an "anything goes" approach to Jewish life, we may lose our uniqueness. I admit this concern is not without merit. However, in a faith that operates without a pope or a Sanhedrin; a religion that is "dogma lite," offering a menu of possibilities on almost every theological position; a religion that has prided itself on its open dialogue and disagreements; and a religion that is really a hybrid with peoplehood, we have to trust that the community itself will develop its own norms, just as we have for centuries. We do not need uniformity in this matter. We do need to trust our people, see-ing diversity as strength, not weakness. I am reminded of Judy Chicago's painting, *Rainbow Shabbat*, in which she depicts a Sabbath table with people of every race and ethnicity, even some of different faiths, all com-ing together to welcome the day of rest. If *shalom* comes from the Hebrew root for "wholeness," then a portrait of our people (and the world) as truly whole and one clearly emerges. I, for one, am inspired by this work and its implications. What are we waiting for?

The world has changed. My parents' generation fought all the battles so that their children could have complete access to any and all of America. And they won! In my time, all the exclusive clubs and neighborhoods, all the quotas limiting our possibilities, and all the stigmas are gone. My sons think of those old realities as ancient history, something they never had to deal with. Today, Jews are wanted, sought after even, seen as beneficial, and desired as friends and partners. Every Jewish *simcha* (celebration) I have attended has a multicultural guest list. Jewish traditions are being incorporated into secular and Christian celebrations. In fact, in this past presidential race in the United States, it was not lost on any of us that *both* candidates had a daughter who married a Jewish man, and it was a total nonissue. Think about it. Despite their vast differences and animosity on the campaign trail, both Donald and Hillary are going to a *seder* this year!

As Tevye declared, "It's a new world, Golde!" Yes, indeed it is. And the answer to the question, "Who is a Jew?" has to change along with it.

• 4 •

Do the Math!

$\mathcal{D}$id you ever wonder what the Jewish community would be like if the Holocaust had never happened? What if the world—instead of ignoring, or even worse, appeasing Hitler—had taken him seriously and stopped him before he got started? Along with North America and Israel, Europe would still be a bustling center of Jewish life. And instead of numbering fifteen million souls, we could probably count at least twenty-five to thirty million Jewish people worldwide. In fact, we are the only ethnic or national group that has not recouped its losses sustained in World War II as there were sixteen million Jews worldwide prior to the war. How can that be?

Now I have never been a quantity over quality person. But I do recognize critical mass and numbers as something we ought not ignore. And with Jewish population in decline everywhere except Israel, we do resemble an endangered species, especially if we are concentrated in one rather dangerous geographical location—namely, the Middle East. While I still believe in the eventuality of regional peace, I am not so naive as to turn a blind eye on those who seek our complete destruction, even annihilation (especially Iran and its proxy "armed to the teeth" terrorist organizations like Hezbollah and Hamas), in that too often volatile region of the world. I mean Ayatollah Khamenei might be kidding when he says, "From now on, in any place, if any nation or any group confronts the Zionist regime, we will endorse and we will help. We have no fear expressing this. . . . The Zionist regime is a cancerous tumor that must be removed, and God willing it will be."[1] Or he may simply be hyperbolic when he states, "The great powers have dominated the destiny of the Islamic countries for years and . . . installed the Zionist cancerous tumor in the heart of the Islamic world. . . . Many of the problems facing the Muslim world are due to the existence of the Zionist regime."[2] Nevertheless, as a people who have faced real genocide throughout our history, I tend to take these threats seriously. Call me overly cautious. I say, better safe than sorry, as long as staying "safe" does not paralyze us into inaction, preventing us from what we need to do for ourselves.

In the face of our decline in numbers as a result of World War II and the Holocaust, as well as the existential threats confronting Israel, the essential and immediate question we need to ask ourselves is this—what do we need to do today so that our numbers will be doubled tomorrow? Like Stephen Covey teaches, "Start with the end in mind."[3] My "end" is a robust, thriving Jewish community of thirty million souls. How do we get there?

Part of the story the Jewish people tell about ourselves is that we were chosen by God. We say we are an *am segulah*, "the chosen people." Now to some that may sound chauvinistic or overly ethnocentric. Many even find it offensive that we think that way at all. I understand that. But "chosen" has *never* meant better. It simply meant we had a special relationship with God as well as a specific task to accomplish.* That task was to live a life of such holiness whereby others would know that there is one God making us one human family on earth. No matter what differences divide us— nationality, religion, language, race, gender, sexual orientation—we are really one. And we need to treat each other with all the respect, love, and dignity that derive from all of us being created equal, *b'tzelem Elohim* (in the image of God). All one has to do is pick up a newspaper (or go online) to realize we are not there yet. Every day we witness acts of hatred and senseless violence, enough to break our hearts. Our "chosen task" has yet to be fulfilled. In other words, we are not done yet; our mission has yet to be accomplished. While this work of making the world a better place for all creatures, for life itself, of course, is not exclusive to the Jewish people, I believe that somehow the world still needs us and the true values of our tradition. That is not a statement of fact. I have no evidence it is true. Lots

---

*I have been told that the names of several Native Americans mean "chosen people" or the "people of God." It is not an exclusive title. Like many families, each child thinks she or he is their parents' favorite. That's good parenting!

of things that are important to us are not "provable," yet we cherish them nonetheless. But I do hold onto this belief of "chosenness" as a motivating factor in my own life, and the life of my people. It motivates me to be a better person and to do my share every day, in every way I can. Hopefully, that's a good thing.

When we hear the word "reincarnation," we do not associate it as a particularly Jewish idea. However, coming out of the Golden Age of Spain, Chaim Vital, the disciple and "secretary" of the Jewish mystic Isaac Luria, collated his master's thoughts on the subject in a work titled *Sha'ar haGilgulim* (literally, The Gate of the Wheels), which has never been translated into English. While much of the work is quite complex, in it he posits that souls return to earth if their work was in some way interrupted or incomplete. While this never became a mainstream Jewish idea for what happens to us after we die, and was rejected by numerous rationalist thinkers, it was picked up on by various Hasidic groups who teach the philosophy to this day. As with many theological concepts—the nature of God, the existence of evil, why bad things happen to good people, for example—Judaism has no single dogma, no "required" adherence to a single concept; rather, it presents us with a "menu" of possibilities, all "kosher," and allows us to form our own, often changing, beliefs. We are a "dogma lite" tradition, emphasizing deed over creed.*

So here is a crazy idea. What if those millions of souls who perished in the Holocaust are already here on earth, people who at present identify with other religions, or no religion at all? I am convinced from the many conversations I have had with colleagues over the years that there is not a rabbi in the world who hasn't had the experience of someone seeking him or her out for conversion and being told some version of, "I never really felt Christian/Muslim, etc. For as long as I can remember, I knew I was born into the wrong body!"

For me, it was studying with Rose M. whose sisters were Cristina and Mary Elizabeth. No joke. When I met her, Rose was a teacher of the Old Testament at the very Catholic parochial school where she herself

---

*It turns out that other rabbinic leaders prior to Luria also believed in the possibility of reincarnation, most notably Moses ben Nahman, commonly known as Nachmanides but referred to as the Ramban. For many reasons, too complex to go into here, all mystical and Kabbalistic thinking was suppressed in the eighteenth century and was not brought back to our attention until the scholarly work of Gershom Scholem in the 1950s and 1960s.

was educated. Rose was a brunette with dark brown eyes; both her sisters were blonde like their mother with eyes the color of a clear blue sky. It took her seven years to complete her conversion! Seven years! Not because she did not know enough; she could have taught almost any Jewish biblical subject. But on some level, her acceptance of her reality felt like a betrayal of those who knew and loved her all her life. It was excruciating for Rose, and I empathized with every painful attempt she made to extract herself. But in the end, she could not continue living what she called a "double life"—one identity on the inside and another on the outside. She was the first, but certainly not the last, experience I had in this regard. Many others followed. People from all over the world sharing this same sense, that against every rational bone in their body, in the face of their family of origin, they are definitively connected to the Jewish people. How very strange, indeed!

So in light of all this, let me ask the only pertinent question. Whether it is reincarnation or some other phenomenon we cannot yet understand, just how many Jewish souls are out there waiting to be recognized?* How many people are living double lives—one faith on the outside and a very different one on the inside? And if this is really the case, then we are not actually converting anyone. Even if we insist on a conversion process (as I do for the sake of worldwide Jewish unity), the bigger truth is that we are merely recognizing a fact they intuited all along and are now welcoming them home.†

We Jews take pride in the fact that we do not proselytize, and that even when someone comes to us for the purpose of conversion we are supposed to turn them away three times to check out their sincerity. After all, if they keep coming back to us, it must be genuine. But it would surprise most of us to learn that those restrictions were imposed on us by the Ro-

---

*I, personally, have a hard time believing that an intact soul transmigrates from one body into another, and I have shared this feeling with my good friend, author of *Many Lives, Many Masters*, Dr. Brian Weiss. Nevertheless, I do believe that what we call "soul" is really life energy, the unique and ephemeral quality in every person that makes us truly us. And since we learn from science that energy cannot be destroyed, merely changed in form, perhaps this energy contains some form of memory as well. Perhaps.

† Back in 2011, I wrote a song to be sung at conversion rituals, titled "I'm Finally Home," to recognize this phenomenon that I believe is prevalent throughout the Jewish world. By the way, what is true in the religious realm is also true of gender identity and sexual orientation. It is as if, in our modern world of choice, people are finding the freedom to go beyond their birth and societal expectations to be their true selves. What a blessing!

mans, only after Constantine announced that Christianity would be the official religion of the Roman Empire. Prior to that, we were quite good at reaching out and bringing in hundreds of thousands of new Jews. And what about the rule that requires rabbis to turn potential converts away? Back in ancient times, the Romans would send spies who pretended to seek conversion. If a rabbi accepted that person, he was reported to the authorities and severely punished, tortured, or killed. We actually created the three rejections rule to protect our rabbis, not to keep potential "Jews by Choice" away!

Turning what was a negative restriction imposed upon us from the outside into some kind of badge of honor, something oppressed minorities often do, from that time forward we made access to Judaism more and more difficult, especially for those of our ancestors who lived in the Christian world. In direct contrast is the approach taken in the code of Jewish law known as the *Shulchan Aruch*. Written by a Sephardic rabbi, Joseph Caro, who had experienced the openness and freedom of the Golden Age of Spain, the *Shulchan Aruch* advises us to keep conversion to Judaism simple and rather quick.[4] When someone comes seeking conversion to Judaism, we should warn them about our history of oppression. And if they say they know about that and still want to be Jewish, we are to "accept them immediately" and only afterward teach them about the principles of Judaism, some of the lighter *mitzvot* (commandments), and some of the harsher ones, but "don't dwell on them." He goes on to describe circumcision and *mikveh* but allows for all kinds of exceptions to the rule. In modern terms, Caro seemed to be lowering all the barriers to Jewish inclusion. In an open society, like the one in which he lived, the attitude that dominated rabbinic thinking was one of ease of acceptance.

Nor was he the first. A famous story is told about the two, often conflictual, colleagues in the time of the Mishna (ca. 110 CE), Rabbi Hillel and his counterpart Rabbi Shammai. According to the legend, a Gentile came to Rabbi Shammai offering to convert to Judaism if he could teach him the entire Torah while standing on one foot. Shammai chased him from his academy with a stick. Somehow undeterred, the same Gentile went to Hillel with the same request. Hillel, balancing on one leg, responded with a version of the Golden Rule, "What is hateful to you do not do to others. That is the whole Torah; the rest is commentary. Now go learn it." So impressed, the Gentile did so and wound up becoming one of the great Jewish scholars of his time. Again, a confident community was a welcoming one. We have much to learn from Hillel's and Caro's examples.

For those of us who have been fortunate enough to work with people during their journey to Judaism, we know that true identity takes years of "doing Jewish" and being part of Jewish communal life. Actually, I used to tell people it would take seven years, a good Jewish number, for the feelings of awkwardness and not really belonging to gradually dissipate and even disappear altogether—seven years for the Jewish way of life and being to feel natural, as if it was always so. Therefore, wouldn't it make sense to lower the barriers to joining and spend more time nurturing converts' growth and full inclusion? Today, it is too often the reverse: high barriers to joining, a meaningful year or more of study and participation, and then relative abandonment once the process of conversion is completed. There are lots of great Introduction to Judaism courses; however, as of 2018, there is no Judaism 201, and there needs to be.

To this day, I receive inquiries questioning if it is possible to convert to Judaism. Sadly, after more than four thousand years of existence, people still do not know that Judaism welcomes those who would join our ranks. After all, our founding mother and father were not born Jews; in fact, given historical reality (not the made-up story of the rabbis about the young Abraham smashing the idols in his father's shop—though it is a classic), they were no doubt polytheists! As a community, we have been overly successful in keeping seekers away. As a result, Judaism remains one of the best kept secrets in the world, and to outsiders, we look like an exclusive club that spurns others. As victims of intense proselytization and even forced conversion, the whole notion of reaching out to others seems distasteful to most modern-day Jews. I understand that. At the same time, I believe the day has come (hopefully it is not too late) for us to amass a worldwide program of actively promoting conversion to Judaism. We need to bring the best minds of rabbis working together with lay business and marketing experts to this project. Given my own experience, and the experience of hundreds of colleagues, I am convinced there are millions of people simply waiting to be asked. We Jews have a well-earned reputation for being good businesspeople. In almost every endeavor, we know how to create success and increase "market share." Can you imagine how well we might do if we turned that attention and effort to sincerely growing the Jewish people?

What might such an effort look like? A marketing campaign using both print and social media would be launched to "welcome people home" to Judaism. There could even be billboards in every major city. A cadre of rabbis and educators would be trained as official guides. Trans-denominational online education in both English and Spanish, especially for those without access to Introduction to Judaism courses, would provide seekers with the necessary learning and tools to live a Jewish life. Communities (synagogues, Jewish Community Centers [JCCs], day schools, Hillel on campus, renewal groups, etc.) would be designated as welcome centers to provide support. Individuals, as well as families, could be trained as mentors and coaches. In other words, this would be a full-on effort of a Jewish community working together for a common purpose—to grow the Jewish people, welcoming true seekers home. Such an energized process will naturally be attractive to others, enhancing public perception of our people and faith, and instead of shrinking, we will grow the Jewish people. For the first time in more than a half century, we will do the math and the numbers will be encouraging! While every Jewish community has benefited from the love and commitment of Jews by choice, I fully understand that not every Jewish leader will get behind such a project. So what! We do not have to be unanimous for this to work—merely unified for a common purpose.* And once it is successful, as I am certain it will be, the recalcitrant will join in the effort.

A previous generation of rabbis also foresaw the problem of a shrinking Jewish community. So what did they do? They encouraged every couple to have at least three children, even four. I am not sure how many listened to these sermons (I do have four sons), but I do know that no matter how well-intentioned they were, my predecessors failed miserably in their goal. We rabbis may have some influence, but, let's be honest, not that much. Growing the Jewish people will not come about as the result of a new baby boom. Talk to your kids. Ain't going to happen. Nevertheless, the goal is still within our reach.

---

*One of my sons was driving past the Bahai Temple in Haifa with a friend who asked him what he knew about their faith. So of course they asked, "Rabbi Google," and the first site enunciated the principles of that beautiful faith tradition. That piqued their curiosity, and they did the same for Islam, Buddhism, and Catholicism; again, the first site had a clear and accessible explanation. They rolled the dice and asked Google about Judaism, and the first site took them to a gift shop selling Jewish ritual objects and *tchotchkes* (kitchy knickknacks). Got to hand it to our people! Talk about being inaccessible!

If you ate at a new restaurant that you really liked, what would you do? You would tell your friends, naturally. You might not even wait to leave the restaurant before you posted pictures of your main course or salad on Instagram or Facebook. You might even join your friends for your next meal there. Most Jews love being Jewish, but they rarely speak about it. Today, throughout the world, there are millions of un-churched individuals who are seeking a spiritual home and are unaware that Judaism even accepts converts.* Let them know. Take them to *shul* (synagogue) with you. Invite them to your home for a Shabbat or holiday meal. Go work out with them at your local JCC. Guess what? This is *not* proselytizing! It is sharing something you love with the people you love. And that has to be a good thing.

---

*I am not the first to use the term "un-churched." The visionary leader Rabbi Alexander Schindler (z"l [literally, "may his memory be a blessing"]) proposed such an effort at a then UAHC (Union of American Hebrew Congregations, now the Union for Reform Judaism) biennial in the 1970s. Though he may have positively influenced some leaders of the Reform movement, his call was largely ignored at best and met with hostility at worst. As on many other issues, Alex was ahead of his time. Today, while the approach to conversion is not hostile (i.e., rabbis don't chase people away), our "effort" can be said to be akin to a retail store on an un-trafficked street that does no advertising and has no media presence but has an old and dusty "Open" sign on its door, and its owner wonders why business is so slow.

· 5 ·

A Funny Thing Happened
to Me on My Way to Miami

$\mathcal{L}$ike many of you reading this, I had thought that the painful chapter of Spain's forced conversion and subsequent expulsion of the Jewish people in 1492, as well as the horrific church-sponsored Inquisition that forced many of our ancestors to keep their precious Jewish faith alive in secret (the so-called *marranos*), was long over.* That is, until I came to serve as

---

*Here is a brief history of the expulsion of the Jews and the Inquisition: In 1492, the same year in which Columbus "discovered" America, King Ferdinand and Queen Isabella of Spain offered the Jews of Spain (then, the largest Jewish community on earth, estimated at two million people) an existential choice. Leave Spain, or convert to Christianity. (Five years later, the Jews of Portugal were given the same "choice.") The reasons behind this ultimatum are too complex to discuss here. Needless to say, the internal crisis that ensued led half of those Jews to leave—to Portugal, Amsterdam, Turkey, North Africa, Italy, Poland, and Safed in Israel—and the other half to ostensibly become Catholics. However, among the *conversos*, there were many who continued to live Jewish lives in secret. And then came the Inquisition, officially created in Spain in the year 1498. Contrary to popular Jewish belief, the Inquisition was not an anti-Semitic effort; rather, it was aimed at rooting out all "false Catholics." The doctrinal efforts of the Roman Catholic Church were being challenged on many fronts. These secret, or crypto, Jews were caught up in the sweep of this web, which, over time, got darker and darker. Neighbors were selling out their neighbors, and so within the Jewish community, children were taught Christian reasons for Jewish practices. This way, if they were questioned, they did not raise any suspicion as to the legitimacy of their Christian faith. Over time, they lost the Jewish connection altogether as it became their "strange" family custom. Other Jews saw a possible escape from this persecution—the New World. But that route was short lived as the Inquisition made it a violation of church law for *conversos* to leave the Iberian Peninsula. When that did not work, the Office of the Inquisition traveled there as well in order to ensure that the Christianity being taught to the natives was strictly in keeping with the doctrines of the church in Rome. Some untold number of crypto Jews escaped into the Andes Mountains or along the Amazon River where the indigenous people were especially hostile to the missionary efforts of the Spaniards, so they found safety. Later, many of these Jews fled to

67

the senior rabbi of Temple Beth Am in Miami. Over the twenty years of my tenure there, numerous individuals from throughout the Latin Americas sought my help in converting to Judaism. While their stories and reasons for doing so were diverse, a familiar thread soon emerged. As they nervously announced to their extended families their intention to throw their lot into the ancient and endless stream of Jewish continuity, someone, their favorite *tio* or *tia*, or a grandparent, would hesitantly inform them of their Jewish roots, often gifting them with a Jewish ritual object that had been in the family for centuries!

For months, I would notice that one of the waitresses who worked for our caterer would stand at the back of the sanctuary during our Shabbat services. Finally, I sought her out to invite her to sit in and be a part of our worship experience. Veronica was born in South America. Raised in the Roman Catholic Church, she was a bit of a rebel, always asking questions, always challenging church doctrine. But even in Venezuela she gravitated to Jewish friends. It continued after moving to the United States. Her boss just "happened" to be Jewish. A neighbor invited her to their Passover *seder*. I asked her if she herself considered conversion, and she replied, "Oh Rabbi, I already feel Jewish. Can I really become Jewish?" Fast forward a couple of years, and it is the morning of her daughter becoming a *Bat Mitzvah*. We gather together, and Veronica wants to show me a gift she received from her aunt on a recent visit home. She opens a box, and in it are two *magen David* stars. I asked, "How nice, where did your aunt buy you these Jewish stars?" It got very quiet in the room. And then Veronica, with tears in her eyes, whispered, "She did not have to buy them. They were my mother's. She left them for me before she passed away. They have been in our family forever." And then the three of us cried as I helped them put on the symbol of their birthright that was theirs all along.

Still, while this piqued my curiosity, I tended to treat it as "interesting anecdotal information" but nothing more. And then I met Carl Hauer Simmonds from Guayaquil, Ecuador. Carl was a senior citizen

---

Central America, Mexico, and eventually across the Rio Grande into New Mexico where their documented descendants today number at least a half million. In modern-day Brazil, it is known that the Amazon town of Recife was the home to those who escaped the Inquisition. Many homes (to this day) still have Jewish symbols carved into their structures, a tribute to the strength of their ancestors. This is true of numerous mountain towns and villages throughout Latin America as well.

who wished to become "officially" Jewish after a lifetime of Jewish commitment. The son of a French Jew who escaped the *Shoa* (Holocaust) in Europe and a Christian Ecuadorian woman, Carl had known no religion other than Judaism. In fact, when he lived in the United States, he was a member of a prominent synagogue in New York City. Nevertheless, especially after the death of his famous journalist father, the local community in Guayaquil (primarily Ashkenazi escapees from Europe) frequently reminded him that he was "not really Jewish." I met with Carl whenever he was traveling to the United States for business or to see his children and grandchildren, and he ultimately completed his return to Judaism with *hatafat dam brit* by a certified Miami *mohel*, immersion in a *mikveh*, and an appearance before a *bet din*.* Over the subsequent years, we stayed in touch. I also had the honor of officiating over his daughter's conversion prior to her becoming a *Bat Mitzvah* in Israel.

Then, one day I received a call from a very distressed Carl. He explained to me that while he was no longer harassed at synagogue, there were "many others" who sought to become Jews but were rejected and turned away by the established Jewish community there. He wanted to rectify that "injustice." I replied by gently suggesting that perhaps at his advanced age he might just want to simply accept the fact (as unfair as it sounded) and be satisfied that he and his daughter were now fully part of the community. Carl would have none of that. "Well, the only other

---

*As a pulpit rabbi, I always insisted that whoever chose Judaism would enter via the traditional standards set by the rabbis hundreds of years ago, and used by all streams of today's Jewish community. After all, people are not converting to a particular rabbi, synagogue, or denominational stream of Judaism. They are converting to Judaism and the Jewish people. These rituals are aimed at mimicking the same rituals parents undertake on behalf of their infant children, for, in fact, in relation to their new faith, they are "like newborns." What are these rituals? *Mikveh*, or immersion in water, represents birth itself. Circumcision on the eighth day of life for males was ordained in the Bible. At the *bris* (as it is popularly known, though the word—the old Ashkenazi pronunciation of the Hebrew *"brit"*—actually means "covenant"), the parents publicly announce for the first time their child's Hebrew name and perhaps talk about the person for whom the child is named (thus keeping memory alive if the person is deceased, as is the custom among many Ashkenazi Jews). This "naming" for converts is done at the *bet din*, or rabbinic court, as the Hebrew name they have chosen is spoken aloud for the first time. Adult males who convert and are already circumcised undergo *hatafaht dam brit*—the taking of a drop of blood from the penis—as a symbolic circumcision. Of course, education is central to the raising of Jewish children. For those who choose Judaism as adults, the learning begins prior to their entry into the community so that they are literally making an educated choice, not one merely on faith alone. Today, a *bris* has become very popular for baby girls as well; thankfully, minus the *milah* or circumcision, of course.

alternative is to start your own synagogue," I sheepishly said. "How do we do that?" was his immediate reply. And so, Bet Jadash Synagogue was born (and is now officially recognized by the World Union for Progressive Judaism). As I had some sabbatical time coming up, I told Carl that I would spend the month of Passover with the community *if* the synagogue was still in existence. And that is where the story gets really interesting.

While I was in Guayaquil—teaching, leading services, hosting the community's first communal Passover *seder*, completing the conversions of the students who spent the year studying (under the direction of an expat who had a Yeshivah of Flatbush education) and living Jewish lives—I was visited by an Israeli named Yaron Avitov from the city of Haifa. How he knew I was in the country I still do not know. Another mystery of the Andes. While living in Israel, Yaron had met an Ecuadorian woman (Masha) who was on a "spiritual quest." They fell in love, and sometime later she asked if he would accompany her back to Ecuador to meet her family. She warned him that her father, who lived in the mountain village of Loca, was called the "taxi driver" because of his poor Spanish. When they eventually met, Yaron thought he heard Hebrew words when speaking to her father, so he asked if he could record him. About a week after sending the tape of their conversation to a linguist in Israel, Yaron received an excited phone call. "The man," the linguist said, "is *not* speaking Spanish. He is speaking Ladino!" (the mixture of Spanish and Hebrew spoken by Sephardic Jews, just as Yiddish, a mixture of Hebrew and German, was to Ashkenazi Jews). When Yaron later asked Masha's father, "Does anyone else speak like you?" he replied, "Nearly everyone in my village!"

Though there is still an element of secrecy for many, this led to Yaron meeting numerous others in the mountain villages of Ecuador (and eventually other Latin American countries) who sometimes reluctantly but always cautiously let him into their homes. (According to Schelly Talalay Dardashti, an expert on Jewish genealogy and the U.S. advisor for MyHeritage.com, "The old *converso* families don't talk about it. As we say in New Mexico, the motto is: 'Deny until you die.'")[1] Yaron was a published author but he felt this experience could only be captured in film, so he went on to create several documentaries. That night I viewed one of them, titled *The Lost Tribe of the Sephardic Jews*. What I saw "blew my mind": dozens of stories of Jewish connections—including one by a Catholic priest, very open and proud of his Jewish heritage—

well hidden for hundreds of years! And that led me to wonder, "So, why are they being revealed now?"

One of the people in the film was Nery Montiel, a rather controversial figure at the time in Guayaquil. Many of the Jews I met in Ecuador thought of him as a "*messianico*," a pejorative term used to describe Christians who were masquerading as Jews in order to convert them to Christianity—what we know in North America as "Jews for Jesus." But none of the people who were disparaging him had ever met him or attended one of his services. I knew I had to do so, and so Carl arranged for a meeting (for which we both got a lot of angry flack).

As we walked into the synagogue known as Bet El Elohai Elohim, we were approached by a slightly built, bearded man with a black *kippah* (Hebrew for *yarmulkah* or skullcap) on his head and *tzitzit* (fringes) visible over his belt. He looked like so many Yemenite Jews I had encountered in Israel. As it turned out, it was Nery Montiel himself. For two hours, I listened to his story, translated by Carl. He had been an Evangelical minister with a large following. Then he had a dream in which a voice said to him, "Save the Jewish people!" Given his calling, he interpreted this to mean that he needed to proselytize Jews, to bring them to Jesus. So he stepped up his efforts. Nery had the same dream two more times. In each successive dream, he felt the anger rise in the voice speaking to him. "I told you to save the Jews!!" Shaken, he decided to seek the help of the family patriarch, his uncle.

"When I told my *tio* the dream, though he is dark skinned like me, he turned white," laughed Nery. And then his uncle revealed the family secret—they were Jews, descended from the *b'nai anusim*, those who were forced to convert at the time of the Inquisition in Spain. His uncle took him out into the field of the family farm and revealed a trap door that led to a large underground room. The room, which served as a small chapel, contained numerous Jewish ritual objects, including a menorah that was dated with Hebrew letters (he later learned) back to the eighteenth century.

It took Nery a few months of deep soul-searching, but with the support of his amazing wife, Linda Macias (who now serves as the cantor of the congregation), he "came out" before his congregation one Sunday morning, announcing his Jewish identity and his desire to turn the church into a synagogue. He told his parishioners, "I understand if you need to leave . . . this is not why you came here. But if anyone wishes to stay, I invite you on this journey with me." About half the church got up and left. But of those who stayed, many had their own secret Jewish stories, or would soon discover them. Nery showed me the *aron hakodesh* (holy ark) they crafted and the Torah scroll they created—a photocopied text from a *chumash* (Torah Commentary), which they glued onto two wooden rollers—because they had no access to a real Torah. Here I was, a Jew from the United States who grew up taking these things almost for granted and was now glimpsing into a world of people who so cherished their Jewish identity that they were willing to sacrifice everything for it. I could not hold back the tears from flowing down my face—an oft-repeated occurrence in working with these brothers and sisters—nor would it be the last time Nery and I cried together.

I have subsequently met those people, as well as the many more who have joined the synagogue and are living observant Jewish lives, often in difficult and isolated situations. Our reach extends beyond Ecuador as others from tiny communities in Chile, Peru, Colombia, Venezuela, and Bolivia have made the arduous and costly journey to Guayaquil when I have been there. It has been my honor to teach there, to join in spirited worship on Shabbat, to officiate at hundreds of conversions, and to create Jewish weddings for many of the already married couples who wish to sanctify their marriage with time-honored Jewish traditions. To be married "in the eyes of God," as they so often say. The incredible stories I have heard and the faces I have seen are deeply etched on my soul. I will never forget the joy, the singing, and the dancing that lasted well into the early hours of the morning on the day I brought them their first kosher Torah scroll. Every person whom I have subsequently brought to the community to witness what is happening under the radar of the Jewish world, no matter their denominational loyalty, says the same thing. "What a privilege to share with them! What an inspiration! I wish I could bottle their enthusiasm and bring it back to my own *shul*."

My travels throughout the cities and mountain villages of Ecuador have provided me with an avalanche of anecdotal information: the *Shechinah* Store selling beauty products; King David's Tavern next door to Miriam's Well grocery (closed on Saturday); and family names, like Levinas or Morales or Medina, which may be rooted in Hebrew (*Levi* was one of the ancient Israelite tribes, *mora* means "teacher," and *medina* is the word for country in Hebrew) and are predominantly found among the crypto Jews.* And then there is DNA. It has been a long-held belief that the indigenous people of the Andes were short in stature. Look around and you will see lots of people measuring less than five feet tall. It turns out that many are carriers of a genetic strain called Laron syndrome. And guess what? The majority of reported cases of Laron syndrome have been in people with Semitic origins, almost all of them being Jews or assimilated descendants of Jews.

Numerous Laron syndrome patients are found in Israel among the country's diverse population composed of Jews from around the world, as well as patients outside Israel originally from communities of the Jewish Diaspora, especially North Africa and the Middle East. There is also a disproportionate number of sufferers found in remote villages of, in all places, Ecuador. Conservative but unsubstantiated estimates indicate that there are more than two million indigenous people with Sephardic Jewish DNA! Who knows how many are living a secret Jewish life? And not just in Latin America. I have heard that in Spain alone, one in twenty Iberian men have genetic markers identifying them as having a Jewish background, while 15 percent of Hispanic men in the Latin Americas have those same markers.†

So why do I insist on a full conversion, then? I do know that the Talmud offers the possibility of a "fast track certificate of return" for those who were forced under dire circumstances to renounce their Judaism. Nevertheless, since there is no real proof of their identity, and because almost all of these lost brothers and sisters have lived as faithful Christians

---

*Early on in Jewish history, the question was asked, "Can we still live a Jewish existence if we are in exile from the Land of Israel?" After all, Judaism, in its origins, was conceived of as a land-based faith—the Land promised to Abraham and Sarah and their descendants. First, prophets declared that we could do so, as exile was a short-term punishment and that we would soon return. Later, the rabbis of the *Kabbalah* posited that while God might be in the Land, God's feminine presence, the *Shechinah*, would travel with us wherever we went, protecting us, keeping us safe. It is interesting, then, that a women's beauty supply shop took the name *Shechinah*. Of course, the proprietor had no idea where the name originated.

† The most popular choice for DNA testing is an autosomal test, which goes back about eight generations and is administered by companies such as MyHeritage, 23andMe, and Ancestry.com. These tests offer a percentage estimate for ethnicity. Beyond autosomal testing, Family Tree, the most popular DNA service for those seeking Jewish roots, offers Y-DNA testing, in which a male can test for his haplogroup, and mtDNA testing, passed along the matrilineal line to both men and women.

for generations with little to no knowledge of Jewish life, I believe a full conversion offers them a true bridge back to our faith and our people. At the same time, I hope to satisfy the needs of the worldwide Jewish community in this regard. After all, it is not me, Terry Bookman, they are joining; it is our people.*

What I have personally experienced in Latin America is taking place throughout the world. Through my work in Ecuador, I have had the privilege of meeting Professor Tudor Parfitt, chair of the Jewish Studies Department at Florida International University. Tudor, a man we might very well call a "righteous Gentile," has made it his life's work to bring attention to the emerging Jewish communities around the globe. He has even testified in Israel's Knesset. Some of the communities he has visited, especially in Africa, trace their Jewish roots back to the first exile, more than twenty-seven hundred years ago!† A recent book by Nathan Devir, *New Children of Israel: Emerging Jewish Communities in an Era of Globalization*, does an excellent job of documenting both the history and current reality in the African continent.[2] Against all odds, by what I can only term a miracle, the spark of Judaism has not been extinguished. And today, in the twenty-first century, we have the almost inconceivable opportunity to fan that spark into a flame. Why can't we do with these brothers and sisters what we did with the Jews of Yemen and Ethiopia? After all, they, too, were cut off from any and all connection to the mainstream Jewish community for generations. And yet, though our attempts at absorption were fraught with problems and serious accusations of prejudice and

---

*Though I know of others who do so, I have never charged any money for my services. I never want anyone to think that I had a financial interest in bringing these folks to Judaism and, therefore, might have overlooked some discrepancy or slipped some people in through the cracks. In fact, the opposite is true. One evening, sitting in the lobby of my small hotel, I was held up at gunpoint. The thief knew exactly where and when to find me. All the hotel staff conveniently disappeared. My friends in the community were convinced that it was organized by the powerful Jews (who do not want to see this happening) in an effort to scare me away. It did not work. I continue to go back and will do so as long as they need me.

† Legend has it that Menelik, the son of King Solomon and the Queen of Sheba, angry and disappointed that he did not inherit the throne from his father, returned to the land of his mother, Ethiopia, and became king there. Whether this is the origin of the Jewish people in Africa is largely conjecture. What is indisputable, however, is the growing claim by millions of Africans that they are, in fact, Jews. Most prominent among them are the Abayudaya of Uganda. Their name, which can be translated as "the people of Judah," proudly displays their blended Jewish African identity: it combines the Bantu prefix "aba-" (people of) with a local pronunciation of the Hebrew name "Yehudah."

worse, in the end, these communities were saved from certain extinction and today have added to the richness and diversity of our people.*

Cynics want to believe that the enormous success of Israel is the catalyst for these people to have suddenly "discovered" their Jewish roots. Often located in the developing world, the argument goes, they wish to seize the opportunity to make *alliyah* under the Law of Return and be supported by the Israeli government. While some of these ancient communities may have kept the dream of returning to Zion as part of their theology and culture (as did my relatives living in Eastern Europe), that has *not* been my experience. The vast majority of the people whom I have helped become Jewish (we now have three synagogues operating in Guayaquil alone) are successfully employed and financially stable with little to no interest in leaving their homes. Some speak of visiting or studying in Israel, but very few wish to settle there. And if a few individuals (or their children) wind up wishing to fulfill the Zionist imperative to dwell in the Land of our ancestors, certainly Israel is well equipped to handle this trickle of newly returned Jews. The last time I was there, I noticed that the lines at the *alliyah* office at Ben Gurion airport were not that long.

Instead, let me offer a narrative more in keeping with reality. What has happened in Latin America is the following: The last fifty years have seen the decline of the once powerful Roman Catholic Church throughout the Latin Americas (with Brazil possibly being one of the few exceptions). When people leave the church, they often are attracted to the growing Evangelical movement sprouting up just about everywhere. Evangelicals (unlike traditional Catholics) have an imperative to study the Bible, especially what they call the "Old Testament." As these Catholic Church "dropouts" start to hear the stories and customs in the books of the Torah, memories are triggered of "strange family practices." And now, with the help of social media, DNA testing services, and the internet, folks are finding out that their so-called strange family practices—cleaning the house for the Virgin Mary every Friday afternoon; not eating bread around Easter; insisting on next day burial for their deceased;

---

*Over the last couple of years, evidence has emerged that an untold number of Jewish babies from these Mizrachi communities were taken from their families and given up for adoption by Jews in the West. This is but one of the ways these communities were persecuted by their Ashkenazi brothers and sisters. Others were "dumped" in so-called development towns that have languished for decades, leading to unemployment, generational poverty, drug addiction, and high crime rates.

fasting one day in September while wearing white clothes and no leather shoes; covering mirrors when mourning a death; pointing to the night sky to notice three stars on Saturday evening (the traditional way to end the Sabbath); sweeping dirt to the center of the floor for no apparent reason— are actually rooted in Judaism.* And this has often led to older relatives confessing the truth—*"We are Jews!"*

This news is life changing. While many happily remain members of the Christian community, the vast majority of those who discover this truth want to know more; some choose complete and full return to the religion and faith of their ancestors, which was cruelly stolen from them more than five hundred years ago. That this spark, this *"pintle Yid"* has been kept aflame all these centuries is nothing short of a miracle. The only question now is this: "Will the organized Jewish community around the world help these brothers and sisters return, or will we be an impediment, closing our eyes to the opportunity this represents for us to recapture the numbers who perished and were lost to us?" Make no mistake about it, millions of people all over the world are discovering the gift which is Judaism. They are taking on a Jewish way of life. Millions more will join them. What will be our response?

One such person in Miami who is trying to make a difference is Genie Milgrom, who came to me seeking conversion a number of years ago. It soon became clear that Genie wanted a more traditional approach to Jewish life, and so I sent her to my Orthodox colleague, Rabbi Israel Becker, who welcomed her with open arms. Genie's subsequent story, after her conversion, is a fascinating one. She has recorded it in a wonderful book, *My 15 Grandmothers*, also available in Spanish as *Mis 15 Abuelas*.[3] After her beloved grandmother died, her mother and aunts informed her

---

*This practice is rooted in the Jewish custom of not disrespecting the *mezuzah* on the frame of each door, as the dirt is swept away from the doorposts. Actually, the word *"mezuzah"* means "doorframe." In the Torah, we are commanded to write "these words" on the doorframe and the gates of our houses. Later Jewish tradition, perhaps because we were forced to move so often, had us write the words on a scroll and then place that scroll in an ornamental container and affix that container onto the doorframe. That container is now called the *"mezuzah"* and continues to be a literal marker of Jewish homes to this day. Some extend the custom to put *mezuzahs* on every doorframe (except the bathroom) in their homes. While not required, it is always okay in Judaism to do more than that which is required, a tradition called *"hiddur mitzvah."* Even though there was no longer a *mezuzah* on their doors, the sweeping practice continued with no explanation other than "This is how we sweep in our family!"

that she would be buried the next day, as is the custom of their family. When Genie protested, since the next day was Shabbat, precluding her as an Orthodox Jew from attending the funeral service, her family ignored her pleas. After the funeral, Genie noticed her mom and aunts marching up the driveway of her home. Thinking she was in trouble for missing her *abuela*'s funeral, imagine her shock when her mother presented her with the gifts her grandmother left for her—including a beautiful *magen David*, a Jewish star! She was Jewish all along, as was everyone in her maternal grandmother's family! Genie's latest project is in helping others make DNA searches more accessible and affordable.

I well realize that any policy that smacks of "proselytizing" is abhorrent to us as Jews; after all, we have been the victims of this disparaging action more times than we can count. But this is not what we are after. These lost family members are knocking on our doors, not the other way around. What "welcome home" are they receiving from us? If my experience is any indication, tragically, they are more likely to be chased away than helped. It is so bitterly ironic that more than seventy years after the *Shoa* in Europe the only ethnic community that has not recouped its numbers is now turning true seekers away!

What official resources are being spent worldwide to discover and recover our lost ancestors? No need to Google. The answer is: practically none. Shavei Yisrael is doing a good job helping those who wish to be Orthodox make *alliyah*, and Reconnector, under the direction of Ashley Perry (former advisor to Israel's minister of foreign affairs), is working with the Israeli government and rabbinate to help individuals return to Judaism. Two small groups in the United States—B'chol Lashon in San Francisco and Kulanu in New York—do great work, but with tiny budgets and minuscule staffs, their impact on these communities, though greatly appreciated, is limited. To date, the worldwide organizations that have the potential to make a difference—like the Joint Distribution Committee, the Hebrew Immigrant Aid Society, the Jewish Agency in Israel, or the American Jewish Committee—have been silent at best or obstructionist at worst. The limited impact that has been made is the result of a handful of dedicated lay volunteers and rabbis who have given their time and resources to make a difference on the ground.

What is needed, then, is a worldwide effort aimed at helping people (re)discover their Jewish roots; an education process that is pluralistic and serves none of the denominational streams; a pathway to conversion that is accessible no matter the observance level; local community leadership training; support and recognition of local communities and their synagogues; and a fair path to *alliyah* for those who choose to live in and serve our Homeland.

After all the tragedies that have befallen our people, it is clear to those of us who have made forays into this world that we have an opportunity that may never come again. Nor is it just a matter of numbers. These lost family members will bring with them the influences of the variety of cultures in which they have survived. They will bring new languages, new dress, ancient traditions, DNA, foods, and music. Just as Jews have always done, they will bring the best of their host cultures with our own particular twist. In short, they will enrich the Jewish experience. But will we be able to open our hearts and minds so as to take full advantage of this opportunity to redefine and expand the Jewish family? Or will we tragically let it slip through our fingers?

Recently, both Spain and Portugal passed laws granting immediate citizenship to any Jew who could prove their family's ancestry went back to the fifteenth century when our people were forced to leave those countries or convert to Christianity. Their descendants, many of whom lived Jewish lives in secret, are the *b'nai anusim*. They live all over the world, and many, perhaps millions, would like to return to the Judaism of their ancestors. Currently their efforts to do so are met with resistance and even hostility. Is it not time to learn from Spain and Portugal and welcome them home?

Our tradition boldly declares that God acts in history as an act of will. While this is not core to my personal theology, I am not so arrogant as to deny the certainty that there are phenomena (like creation itself) that may never be fully explained away by science. Nonetheless, more often, I am a proponent of the idea that God acts in the world through human beings, through us. I am also not one of those people who believe that we can look into the Bible as a predictor of the future. I don't think of prophets as "seers" prognosticating all that will befall humankind; rather, they were powerful and courageous individuals who looked honestly at their society and its leadership, reminding us that all of our actions have consequences. With their prose and poetry, themselves lifted up by the "voice of God," which they "heard" in the core of their being, they inspired generations to strive to be better people, just as they do today. Nevertheless, each year, as the Torah cycle draws to a close, when I read the following words it gives me pause: "Adonai will scatter you among all the peoples from one end of the earth to the other . . . yet even among these nations you will find no peace" (Deut. 28:64–65).

A horrible punishment, if ever there was one. The intended plan was one people living peacefully in one Promised Land, serving their one God. Yet if you look at the totality of Jewish history, that plan had a very short shelf life. In fact, for most of our history the Deuteronomy passage held sway and was even "prophetic." We were scattered and despised everywhere we went. True, there were moments of great wealth and prosperity—the Talmudic period in Babylon; the Golden Age of Spain; and intermittent but short-lived special status in numerous lands, especially the Islamic and Ottoman Empires throughout North Africa, the Middle East, and what is now Turkey, as well as the contemporary United States of America—but for much of our history, insecurity and uncertainty was the rule of thumb.

But just as we are about to lose hope, we read in the following week's *parsha*:

> When all of these things befall you amidst all the nations to which Adonai your God has banished you . . . then Adonai your God will restore you and take you back in love. Even if your scattered are at the ends of the world, from there Adonai your God will gather you, from there fetch you and bring you back. (Deut. 30:1–5)*

Three times God is called by the intimate name YHVH (the ineffable name that by tradition we pronounce Adonai); three times we are reminded that this is "your" God.† The relationship, no matter how extenuated and seemingly lost, the Torah reminds us, is nevertheless eternal. It

---

*In many synagogues, this passage is read on Yom Kippur, our annual day of atonement and renewal of the relationship both with the community and with God. The metaphor is apt as for many modern Jews the High Holy Days serve as a type of once-a-year pilgrimage. Actually, in ancient times, prior to synagogue life, when there was a Temple in Jerusalem, probably the only time many people were able to connect was also once a year, on one of the festivals. It was only after the advent of the synagogue did attendance at worship services become a regular, everyday occurrence.

† Rabbi Lawrence Kushner once suggested that since this God name is composed of four vowels, saying it is really like breathing. And since *neshamah*, the Hebrew word for soul, comes from the root for "breath," all three are interconnected—God's name, our soul, and our breath.

can be abrogated and damaged but never completely broken. And no matter how far apart we may be and no matter how long we may have been out of touch (literally off the grid), God remembers us, loves us, wants us to be in relationship, and so will bring us back to "Himself" and to our Land of Promise. When I reflect on these passages, I cannot help but image two lovers whose volatile relationship causes numerous breakups, but in the end, they find they are unable to live without one another.

Now this may not be your personal theology. You may not think of God in this way. You may not think of God at all. But even from a purely peoplehood perspective, our biblical text reminds us that we are forever united as *b'nai Yisrael* (the children of Israel). Despite our many differences in the way we look, speak, and observe (or choose not to do so), we are, in fact, one family sharing a common destiny. Despite the numerous lands and cultures in which we have made our "temporary" home, we really have only one home. We Jewish people are, for better and sometimes worse, likewise connected throughout history and for all eternity.

One has to wonder, in regard to the return to Zion that began in the nineteenth century as well as the emerging Jewish communities—a phenomenon we are witnessing literally all over the globe—is this the predicted ingathering spoken of in our Torah? For even if it is not, even if the Torah text was speaking of a much more current and localized happening, the similarity is inescapable. The prayer of our people, chanted three times daily in every place we have ever been (and we have been just about everywhere on earth)—*l'kabetz g'looyotaynoo . . . may'arbah kanfote ha'aretz* (gather our exiles from the four corners of the earth)—has the potential to be answered. Today. Now. And not only from the four corners, but every space and place in between.

Along those same lines, there are groups throughout the world that claim Jewish ancestry dating as far back as the first exile, centuries before the Common Era. Every exile since created the current Diaspora. Has it not been our fervent hope—recorded in the holy words of our Torah, prayed for every day in our *siddur* (prayer book), and just as we take up the four *tzitzit* from the corners of our *tallit* into our one hand—to gather our exiles from the ends of the earth? Has not the State of Israel been called *reisheet geulah*, the beginning of our redemption? Well, guess what? They are ready to come home. To our Land. To our people. Now we really have to ask ourselves, "What, if any, will be their welcome?"

· 6 ·

Love versus Loyalty

$\mathscr{I}$t has been said that if you want to know what the chief concerns of the Jewish people are, look at the sermons rabbis are preaching. I am not sure that is always correct, but at the very least, we can know what the concerns of the rabbis are. If we examine those sermons in the decades of the 1970s through the 1990s, as well as the conversations held at gatherings of the Jewish Federation's General Assembly and other Jewish communal organizations, intermarriage was probably the number one topic leaders chose to address. And back then, the typical attitude was one of alarm coupled with extreme opposition. For example, at the forty-third annual gathering of the Rabbinical Council of America at the Pineview Hotel in Fallsburg, New York, on June 19, 1979, then president Bernard Rosenzweig declared that intermarriage had reached "catastrophic levels," announcing that he had formed a commission to fight it. He went on to say that the "problem" was particularly severe among college youth, constituting "a serious threat to Jewish communities and the survival of traditional Judaism." Rabbi Rosenzweig concluded by declaring, "We must not become tolerant of this cancerous growth which can only destroy Jewish ranks."[1]

Back then, rabbis and Jewish leaders alike thought that if we just got the right message through—that "each intermarriage drives a nail in the coffin of Judaism," or that intermarriage was the "silent Holocaust" destroying the Jewish people—we could stem the tide and young Jews

81

would choose tribal loyalty over love.* Wrong. As the percentage of intermarriage continued to rise despite communal and rabbinic opposition, the battle only intensified. The metaphorical alarm was sounded with the 1990 National Jewish Population Survey reporting that at least half of all Jews were marrying "out of the faith."[2] A consensus formed around the belief that if this trend was not reversed, the whole fabric of the Jewish communal structure would suffer irreparable damage. Jewish groups then poured millions of dollars and untold human resources into efforts to stem what was seen as a threat to the very future of the Jewish community. All those efforts were for naught as the intermarriage rate held steady and continues to do so. What the Jewish world has failed to understand is that we lost the battle because we actually won the war against exclusion, anti-Semitism, and hatred. But in the process, we may have lost the better part of a generation of Jews who felt disparaged, ostracized, and rejected—veritable "traitors" to the cause of Jewish continuity. While it may be too late to bring them back, there is no reason we need to add to these losses. None.†

Every Jewish population survey over the last few decades indicates that the intermarriage rate among Jews is somewhere around 50 percent. That is to say, since the 1970s, for almost fifty years, nearly one out of every two Jews marries out of the faith. But that belies the real numbers. First, that statistic derives only from those who identify with the Jewish

---

*Actually, the first person to coin the phrase "each intermarriage drives a nail in the coffin of Judaism" was a Reform rabbi, David Einhorn, in the nineteenth century. My first response in hearing it was, "I did not know that Judaism was dead, and ready to be buried!" Similar sentiments have been expressed in the decades that followed. Though we are uncertain of the origin of the term, Rabbi Ephraim Buchwald of the National Jewish Outreach Program is often associated with calling intermarriage the "silent Holocaust."

† In addition to making the intermarried feel unwanted, in the 1960s and 1970s, when I was growing up for the second time, Jews seeking greater spirituality were driven away from synagogues and Jewish organizations as if their desire was somehow "un-Jewish." We were treated as pariahs, and so many left the fold, finding a spiritual home in forms of Buddhism or with gurus from Yoga and Hinduism. We literally exported hundreds of thousands of our youth who, wounded by their experience in the Jewish world, have never returned. Those of us who managed to stay, thanks to the efforts of individuals like Rabbi Shlomo Carlebach (to whom I was introduced by my fallen-away Orthodox Jewish Yoga teacher) and Reb Zalman (who actually wrote back to me after I had written him upon reading his first book and became a lifelong mentor) were instrumental in leading the way to alternative Jewish formats like the Chavurah movement. By the way, both of these flawed but courageous rabbis were shamefully excoriated by the Jewish establishment in their time.

community, and we know not every born Jew does. Second, the statistic includes Orthodox Jews as well. Though they represent only 10 percent of the total Jewish population, their intermarriage rate is understandably far lower as the social pressure for endogamy in these tight-knit, highly structured communities tends to be a lot stronger. In fact, the intermarriage rate among "liberal" and unaffiliated Jews may be as high as 71 percent according to the most recent Pew Research Center population survey (2013).[3]

However, a much better way to understand what has been truly happening in the American Jewish community (as well as all the other Diaspora communities) is the following illustration. If we put ten marriageable age Jews in a room, four of them will choose a Jewish partner while six of them will marry someone of another faith. In other words, for every ten Jews, we are creating two Jewish families and six interfaith families! While, of course, some of the latter group will choose conversion to Judaism, thereby creating more Jewish families, those numbers remain quite low. And solely from a DNA perspective, in just one generation we have radically altered the gene pool of the Jewish people.* Just take one look at the children in any Jewish Community Center or synagogue preschool or day school. We are no longer a homogenous collection in which everyone "looks Jewish" (i.e., "looks like me"). We have a lot of blond and blue-eyed children singing "Shabbat shalom" and the *motzi* (the blessing) over bread before they eat.

By and large, the so-called Jew in the street has accepted this new reality, though the organized Jewish community, especially traditional rabbis, has not. Very early in my rabbinic career I was asked to address a Hadassah group. The topic was "Will my grandchildren be Jewish?" I asked the group, "How many of you have a significant family member who is not Jewish?" Several hands went up. Ten years later, that same group extended me another invitation to address the same topic. Again, I asked the question. Almost every hand went up. And though there was concern and ambivalence about the greater issue of the collective Jewish future, not one woman there said she was willing to lose her personal

---

*Medical science tells us that Jewish genetic diseases, partially due to increased genetic testing and partially due to fewer carriers, are markedly down. In other words, in this case, intermarriage has had a beneficial effect on our genetic health. There is a delicious irony in that fact.

relationship with her non-Jewish or "half Jewish" grandchildren.* No one was going to "fall on their sword" in order to make a point. It is true that, from the rabbinic side, the futile sermons have decreased and the topic of intermarriage rarely makes it onto the current communal agenda as a problem to be solved. But has the attitude really changed? Of course, most committed Jews I know would prefer that their children marry within the faith, for cultural as well as religious reasons. They want their *machatunim* (the parents of their son-in-law or daughter-in-law) to be members of the tribe, to share the same values, traditions, and similar life journeys. We can understand that. Nevertheless, the organizational Jewish world continues to see intermarriage as an obstacle. What if we decided to change the context of the discussion and treat it as an opportunity? I know that idea might sound counterintuitive, even radical. However, context is always decisive.†

Perhaps a short historical excursus might be helpful at this point. Given the enmity we see in modern times toward exogamy in the establishment Jewish community, we might think Judaism has always forbidden intermarriage. However, contrary to what one might think, the Bible is not so clear-cut in this matter. In fact, studying our sources, we might ask this question: Does Jewish law prohibit or rather discourage intermarriage? Rabbi Avram Mlotek, a graduate of Yeshivat Chovevei Torah, provocatively suggests that such an examination of our sources ought to lead us to "rethink our resistance to intermarriage."[4] Remember, the first Jews, Abraham and Sarah, grew up as polytheists, worshipping many gods

---

*According to the 2013 Pew Research Center study, only 20 percent of interfaith couples say they are raising Jewish children. Since the true intermarriage rate is holding steady at around 60 percent, there are probably close to a million children in the United States alone who would say they are "part Jewish" or have a Jewish parent, though they do not self-identify as Jewish. In other words, those Hadassah women have lots of non-Jewish grandchildren to love.

† To understand what I mean here, think of context as background. When we change the background, that which is in front also changes. My artistic director son demonstrated this to me in an empty theater one time. Just by changing the lighting, everything on stage, including the words being spoken, was altered. We do the same in language. When I call something a problem, people's listening is attuned to solving it or fighting it. When I call it an opportunity, the listening is around possibility and a desire to join in. This is one you can try at home.

Here's a cute story: Two Israeli bounty hunters are out looking for terrorists. They make camp for the night. In the morning, Yoam crawls out of his tent, stands up to stretch, and realizes they are surrounded by terrorists armed to the teeth. He rushes back into his tent and cries out, "Nissan, we're rich!" Context.

and their idols. In effect, by accepting Adonai as their exclusive God, they were converts. When it came time for Isaac to marry, Abraham sent his servant to the "old country" to find him a wife, but that decision had nothing to do with religion per se, since Rebecca, too, was an idol worshipper. Yes, Esau marries Hittite women, which (perhaps) disgusts his mother, leading to a ban against marrying any Canaanite woman, but that seems to be more about proximity than religion. In other words, since these ancestors of ours, proto-Jews, were alone in their faith, the concern was the potential influence or peer pressure the other surrounding religions might have. I say this because our heroes Joseph marries an Egyptian, Moses marries a Midianite, King David and King Solomon have many foreign wives, and, after the first exile in the sixth century BCE, Ezra the Scribe returns and demands that Israelite men divorce their foreign wives, so widespread was the practice. In other words, the prohibition against exogamy was limited, and the concern had more to do with the influence a host culture (them) could have on a minority community (us) than on religion per se. When we were the majority, as in the time of our monarchy when we exercised sovereignty over our laws and communal destiny, the concern seems to have largely disappeared.

I witnessed that firsthand when I lived on a *kibbutz* (communal settlement) in Israel. Foreign Christian volunteers from Europe were absorbed into the community, spoke Hebrew, celebrated Shabbat and holy days, and often married *kibbutzniks* without the benefit of any formal conversion. It was natural and easy. And in some ways, it felt very similar to the Torah status of *ger toshav* (resident or temporary alien; similar to a person with a green card).* Later on in Jewish history, of course, the prohibition against intermarriage was expanded to include all Gentiles. When? In Babylonia when, once again, we were a minority surrounded by a host culture with a different faith. So if we want to be honest with ourselves we need to ask some difficult questions. Is the prohibition against "marrying out of the faith" really a religious issue? Or is it a matter of assimilation? And if we took the "fear of assimilation" off the table (i.e., the Jewish partner maintains his/her Jewish identity and commitment), is it really still a serious problem?

---

*The *ger toshav* is frequently mentioned in the Torah, beginning in the Book of Exodus 12:45. While understood that they were not Israelites, they were subject to many of the responsibilities and had access to numerous privileges of Jewish identity.

Once upon a time and not so very long ago, to marry "out of the faith" meant a rejection of Jewish identity and a desire to leave the community behind. Marrying out meant marrying up in society and personal status. That's not true today. As Rabbi Adina Lewittes, former assistant dean at the Jewish Theological Seminary, writes,

> There was a time when it was very clear that if somebody chose to marry somebody who wasn't Jewish, they understood the consequence was to be pretty much marginalized [if not excommunicated] from their Jewish community. Now marrying someone who is not Jewish is not an expression of their diminishing desire to stay rooted in their Jewish lives and values. It's something they've experienced as being entirely consistent with who they understand themselves to be as Jews.[5]

In other words, our children fully get that accepting, even loving, the "other" is a true expression of the Jewish values they were taught and that to not do so feels like racism, or cultural chauvinism, or even bigotry. Our children, by and large, see no conflict in being Jewish *and* being married to someone who is not. Their identity is individual (a topic I discuss in greater detail in chapter 3, "Who Is a Jew?"), not communal or tribal.

I remember a childhood song we used to sing to tease a friend when they acknowledged a girlfriend or boyfriend. "X and Y sitting in a tree, K-I-S-S-I-N-G, first comes love, then comes marriage . . ." We did not realize it back then, but the song represented a radical shift in human relations. Until the modern era, and still persisting in some contemporary cultures like India and large swaths of the Muslim world, parents arranged for their children's marriages. Back in those days, first came marriage, and then hopefully love. Recall Tevye's question to Golda, "Do you love me?" And her ultimate answer, "I suppose I do." Modernity changed the way people coupled. Today our kids "fall in love" and then, perhaps, get married. In modern times, love has become the primary basis for all marriage. Today, and only for about the last two hundred years of human history, we somehow believe that our children are the best decision makers for their future life partner because they and only they can determine who it is they love.

Actually, the challenge to the traditional family structure blossomed with the dawn of the modern era, the end of the eighteenth century, and Napoleon's conquest of Western Europe, which brought the philosophy of the French Revolution to what was then called "the civilized world." All hierarchical relationships were upended and called into question as each person attained the freedom to make their own decisions and control their own destinies. Life, liberty, and the pursuit of happiness became our in-alienable rights as human beings. Less than a century later, as the *Haskala*, or Enlightenment, reached Eastern Europe, Sholom Aleichem wrote his *Tevye the Dairyman* series of short stories. Before it was turned into the sensational musical smash in both theater and film, this book was actually a very serious questioning of societal and family norms as well as restric-tions in a fast-paced, changing world. Tevye and Golda's eldest daughter Tzeitel rebels against her arranged marriage to Lazer Wolf the butcher because she is in love with Motel. What is really radical in the story is that she gets her father to go along with it, choosing a modern-day norm over the much vaunted tradition. Their second daughter runs off with her boyfriend, the revolutionary, without the benefit of marriage, and at the railway station, Tevye gives his blessing to them both. The third daughter wishes to marry a Gentile, and here is where Tevye draws the line. He has gone far, but in the latter part of the nineteenth century, that is too far for him. Tradition can bend but not be broken. I would argue that as a Jewish community, we have long since passed Tevye's proverbial line in the sand. We have accepted the reality that our children will marry out of the faith. Now, we need to take that to the next level as well.

We could point to the high divorce rate and say that love marriage is not working out so well, but I am not so sure that is a great measure of marital success. After all, in those cultures in which parents arrange their children's marriages, divorce is frowned upon and discouraged. Couples who choose to end their unhappy marriages are often disparaged, even ostracized, or worse. And for those couples who choose to stick it out, we have no way of knowing if any of those marriages are personally fulfilling, though I hope they are. But even if we did, in this day and age, there is no way the vast majority of our children are allowing us to pick their spouses. We are lucky if they ask us, "So what do you think?" For better or worse, culture shifted, and the world changed. We send our kids out into that world trusting that somehow they will know who is right for them. And how will they know? They will "fall" in love.

So why is it that Jewish parents still balk or feel some sense of failure and embarrassment when their son or daughter happily announces that they have fallen in love with a person of another faith? Why do we still see this as some betrayal of the tribe? Did we teach them that tribal loyalty must triumph over love? And even if we did, does anyone really believe that in a free society this message can really work? Of course, we know that two Jewish parents are more likely to produce Jewish children who, in turn, will produce more Jewish children. No one can deny that. Every study has unequivocally demonstrated that. And for those of us who are concerned about the Jewish future, it makes perfect sense to want our children to find and fall in love with a Jewish boy or girl. Besides, marriage is difficult enough without this cultural difference to overcome. But all of this desire on our part falls apart in the face of our new reality. And when parents who have displayed little Jewish connection "go nuts" because their child wants to marry a person of another faith, that child is completely dumbfounded. I know. They have come to me too many times to count saying something like, "Rabbi, I don't understand. We never celebrated Shabbat. Passover *seder* was a joke. My parents dragged us to synagogue once a year. We were hardly Jewish! We even had a Chanukah bush and got Christmas presents when I was a kid. I have been to Israel while they are still waiting for it to be safe. And now they are going all holy-roller on me! I don't get it!" And while I try to explain this is not a rational thing for their parents, it is difficult for me to understand it as well.

So let's backtrack a moment and talk about that world into which we send our children. It has been said that we live in the most open and democratic society in the history of the world. This is true both in North America as well as Europe. Even for our children who attend Jewish day school, their opportunities to meet and become friends with children from different backgrounds and faiths is practically unlimited. Whether it is in Little League baseball, gymnastics camp, Judo lessons, summer camp, neighbors, Boy Scouts and Girl Scouts—you name it, multicultural environments abound. And we haven't even arrived at college yet.

With few exceptions, the values our children are taught—respect for others, pluralism, acceptance of differences, equality—all lend themselves to the deep understanding that all people are created in the image of God, and no one is better than anyone else because of their race, gender, sexual orientation, or religion. American Jews especially believe that there are no conflicts between their Jewish values and their human values, and we teach that to our children. One can be a good American and a good Jew.

And being a good Jew means accepting all others as equals, no matter our differences. To think or feel otherwise is to be a bigot. We are proud that our children have friends from all walks of life, as well we should be. And so it seems to them that we go literally crazy when they bring home a partner from another faith. They have a point.

In 1994, *Lilith* magazine featured a cover story that challenged our thinking on this matter. The premise of the story was how incredible and unlikely it is that, given the openness of our society, about half of our children still chose a Jewish partner![6] The story was not well received by the Jewish establishment. But they had a valid point in their attempt to turn the argument on its head. The proverbial half-full cup!

I will take it a step further. The fact that our children are able to fall in love with and marry anyone of their choosing is a sign that we have been more successful than our grandparents could have ever imagined. In 2010, the marriage between Chelsea Clinton and Marc Mezvinsky prompted a debate over whether to celebrate the extent of Jewish inclusion in the corridors of American power, or lament yet another soul lost to the community. The fact that in the 2016 U.S. presidential election *both* candidates had a Jewish in-law child and grandchildren who are being raised Jewish, and no one batted an eye, is little short of a modern-day miracle. Our parents' generation fought against anti-Semitism and discrimination that limited our choices as well as our opportunities. They won that war. Today Jews can enter any profession or university. We live where we want and with whom we want. There are no quotas and zero barriers to our full involvement as well as inclusion in any and all aspects of society. We should be celebrating, not wringing our hands!

As Naomi Schaefer Riley writes, over the past half century intermarriage has become increasingly common in the United States among *all* religions—but among Jews, at one of the highest rates.[7] Why is that? There are several factors. First is the decline, even absence, of Christian opposition. We forget that once upon a time it was forbidden, even illegal, in some places for a Christian to marry a Jew! That began to change when, in 1807, Napoleon's Grand Sanhedrin declared that all such marriages were valid. A few decades later, in 1844, this ruling was extended by the Rabbinic Conference of Brunswick, as long as the children were not prevented from being raised as Jews. Second, as our numbers decline as a percentage of the total population, our children have less access to other

Jews. As a pulpit rabbi in Miami, I saw far fewer intermarriages than I did when I was in Milwaukee. Bigger Jewish communities provide more opportunities to meet other Jews. Plain and simple. Later marriage is a third factor. As people age, and the biological clock starts ticking loudly, the religion of our potential partner becomes a lower priority. Fourth, higher education also is a factor. People with advanced degrees are more likely than their peers with less education to not want children. When children are taken out of the equation, religion declines as a factor in one's future mate. Finally, greater freedom and emphasis on self-determination weakens the hold of the community's power and desires. Whenever our people experienced true freedom, intermarriage rates have gone up. Intermarriage is not new in our people's history. Nor is it new in the United States. During the colonial era, Sephardic Jews, a small minority population perhaps as few as 50,000 people, were largely absorbed into the general population and had all but disappeared by the early nineteenth century.

Here are the facts. Unless we are willing to return to a self-imposed ghetto, or *shtetl*, our children will fortunately interact with children of various faiths and diverse backgrounds. Inevitably, because we send them off as young, sexually active adults to find their way in the world, many of them will fall in love with one of those kids we taught them to think of and treat as an equal—those same kids with whom they went to school; celebrated birthdays, communions, and *Bar/Bat Mitzvahs*; and shared Shabbat and holidays, including Christmas and Chanukah as well as Passover and Easter. That is what the intermarriage rate should be teaching us. That is what is happening on the ground of real life. Our choice, our only choice, is how we will respond. I suggest that we react by being the most loving, accepting, best Jewish in-laws we can possibly be. For then, and only then, will our in-law child of another faith learn that Judaism is a warm and welcoming tradition. After all, let's not forget, our founding mother and father, Sarai and Avram (as they were called before life and God would change their names and fate), were not born Jewish either.

Last year my partner and I attended a wedding in California in which the bride was Jewish and the groom was not. As a pulpit rabbi, I officiated at many weddings (including co-officiation with judges and other clergy at interfaith weddings) but rarely stayed for the celebration afterward. Here I was a guest. What totally impressed me were the friends of the bride and groom. They were from every background possible—Indian, African, Asian, Hispanic, Caucasian—and every faith. And yet, they were all totally comfortable, as well as knowledgeable, in this Jewish setting. You should have seen them dance the celebratory dance of the *horah*! They even said the "ch" in *l'chaim* correctly! But beyond that, they were amazing young people—smart, accomplished, gracious, easy to talk to—the kinds of people and friends with whom one hopes his or her children will connect.

What I gleaned from that wedding as well as my thirty-five years in the "rabbi business" is that while we can continue to behave as if intermarriage is an obstacle to Jewish continuity, it really is an opportunity. Seeing how welcoming we are, some will choose to accept Judaism as their own faith; others will be supportive of raising Jewish children. At the very least, we will make friends for the Jewish community. For how can our *machatunim* and extended family from other faiths harbor any ill will toward us when their grandchildren, nieces, and nephews have 50 percent Jewish DNA? In point of fact, while at one time our non-Jewish neighbors would have seen marrying a Jew as a negative (what is the Christian version of the embarrassing scandal we call *"shandah"*?) today they see it as a blessing. They take pride in the fact that they now have Jewish relatives. They happily attend Jewish worship and life cycle events. They come with true curiosity and openness to Jewish holiday celebrations. They are genuinely touched when allowed to participate. I know. I have witnessed it too many times to count. They even join Jdate to actively seek a Jewish marriage partner. As the sociologists Robert Putnam and David Campbell conclude, in today's America we are more likely to see philo-Semitism than anti-Semitism.[8] Despite the few haters who grab all the attention and headlines, diverting our energy and resources, America loves its Jews! Isn't that great news?

Sadly, despite all the evidence, our thinking and behavior in the Jewish world vis-à-vis intermarriage has really not changed that much in the last fifty years. While some of us, unwilling to sit *shivah* for and disconnect from our children (and grandchildren) have reluctantly accepted the reality, still, our attitude is one of loss and maybe even some shame. In our collective *kishkes* (guts), if we are being truly honest, we feel rejected by our children; we feel we must have done something wrong. And if, "God forbid," our children actually convert to their spouse's faith, we are devastated. But as the Pakistani Muslim protagonist of the film *The Big Sick* said to his parents when they discovered he was in love with a white American girl, "What did you expect when you brought me here?" I say to my coreligionists and all members of the tribe, "Did you think we could acquire all the 'goodies' of American life and still live fiddlers on the roof?"

By the way, my Orthodox-all-her-life *bubbe* used to remind me that if all was so good back there in "*Anatevka*" none of them would have ever left. Life was by and large pretty miserable and dangerous for our people, especially in Eastern Europe and Russia.

In an open society, intermarriage is an inevitability. Or as Emma Green writes in a most provocative article focusing on the Conservative movement, "The challenge of intermarriage . . . is not going away. The question has been called."[9] Now we need to respond in a way that is good for our children and good for the Jews. As my Talmud teacher at Hebrew Union College Rabbi Michael Chernick taught us, "When there is a rabbinic will, there is a *halachic* way!" As radical as this may sound, instead of looking at intermarriage as a loss, we need to think of it as a win. Yes, we lost the battle against intermarriage; given historical realities, there could have been no other outcome. But we won the war. We have won our equality. We have won our status. We have won our full acceptance. These were hard-fought battles. And if we come to see this as a positive development, then we will win our children's ongoing connection to the people and faith that nurtured them all of their lives. The families they create and the traditions they incorporate will look a bit different than the ones in which we grew up, but those differences can also come to be seen as a positive development in the long and always interesting journey of our Jewish people.* For here is the real choice before us. If not accepted and embraced, intermarriage has the potential to diminish our community, marginalize our children and grandchildren, and even separate us into two or more people. It all depends on the perspective we choose to take.

---

*In chapter 12, verse 38 of the Book of Exodus, we learn that an "*erev rav*" (mixed multitude) went up out of Egypt. While the Torah does not define exactly what this means (and later blames some of the rebellious behavior on them), I imagine it implies that not everyone who chose to leave Egypt and join their fate with that of the Children of Israel were, in fact, descendants of Jacob. And yet somehow, after forty years of wandering, they became one people. That is an exact parallel to the communal opportunity we have today. Can we make room on the bus for our half Jewish and non-Jewish family? As I wrote earlier, when I lived on a *kibbutz* in Israel, there were volunteers from Europe who were of other faiths. Yet somehow, over time, they were absorbed without fanfare into the community. They were sort of modern-day *gerim*—true members of the community who were not Jews. Substantially, we have created this situation de facto in the Diaspora. Perhaps it is time to recognize this as fact as has been suggested by several rabbis (Rabbi Geela Rayzel Raphael, Rabbi Amichai Lau-Lavie, and Rabbi Steven Greenberg among them) that reinstituting this category might be a proactive way to creatively deal with intermarriage and wedding officiation today.

Is the Synagogue (and All Other Jewish Institutions) Really Dead?

Though the synagogue is more than two thousand years old, and rabbis have held sway for approximately the same amount of time, we were not always organized this way. According to the story we tell, we began as a single family; somehow grew in number while in Egyptian slavery; and were led through the wilderness and into the Land of Promise by two charismatic leaders*—Moses (lawgiver, judge, ruler, and military general) and then Joshua (military general and ruler)—plus Aaron (and then his sons) as high priest or religious leader.

After settling in the Land, we were loosely organized as tribes led by judges and priests; eventually created a monarchy and a centralized Temple; and were chastised as well as goaded to greater fidelity to God by prophets. After a seventy-year exile (about which we know very little) reconstituted by scribes—Ezra and Nehemiah—we rebuilt the Temple and were led again by priestly families and "governors." Only toward the end of the Temple period (approximately eighteen hundred years since our founding mother and father began their journey to the Land of Promise, according to the traditional accounting) did the synagogue—led by rabbis who were teachers, interpreters of Torah, and political leaders—emerge. In other words, for almost two millennia we organized ourselves while impacting the world without the benefit of either a single synagogue or rabbi.†

---

*We tend to think of charisma as "charm" or "force of personality," but in the biblical sense, it means a divinely conferred power or talent.

† The word "rabbi" is composed of two Hebrew words—*rav* and *sheli*—"master" and "my." Hebrew attaches possessive pronouns to the end of nouns. Literally, rabbi means

While at one time it was thought that the synagogue came into existence only after the Temple in Jerusalem was destroyed by the Romans in the year 70 CE, archeologists have confirmed that synagogues existed prior, perhaps as early as the second century before the Common Era. Evidence of a Hasmonean synagogue somewhere between Modi'in and Latrun; in Migdal, Capernaum, and Herodium; and the Delos synagogue all demonstrate that the movement away from hereditary priesthood and sacrificial offerings was well under way. Though it is beyond the scope of this work to speculate as to why that was happening, and indeed there were many forces at work—political and economic as well as religious— suffice to say the belief in the efficacy of such a system was sufficiently eroded and a new system was needed to take its place. And though the theology of the Jewish people continues to hold onto the notion of a return to the Temple in Jerusalem, literally prayed for in the traditional *siddur* morning, noon, and night, I would venture to say that the vast majority of the global Jewish people are not particularly anxious to bring their favorite pets to be slaughtered and offered up by a *Kohen* (priest) on the altar of God. In fact, if there is reincarnation, I hope I led a good enough life to come back as a Jewish pet.

Though it will probably be very difficult to understand for anyone like myself who has grown up in the twentieth century, the synagogue itself was an innovation. It was created by a group of individuals collectively known as the Pharisees who were attempting to adapt to a changing environment and belief system. Their innovation turned out to be prophetic, for had they not come up with the notion that the synagogue would become a tripartite house of gathering, study, and prayer, and that each private home would become a *mikdash m'at* (a small sanctuary) with our kitchen table the new altar and the *challah* (bread) the new symbolic "sacrificial offering," perhaps we, the Jewish people, would have died out altogether.* In other words, these Pharisees radically altered the way we "do Jewish," while making it look like it was the Torah's intention all along, and got away with it! Prayer three times a day, acts of *gemilut hasa-*

"my master" in the sense that masters were teachers (like a headmaster is in charge of the school or the leader of all the other masters).

*The literal meaning of *challah* is the "portion of dough" that was offered up and burned as a ritual sacrifice; only later did it come to mean the festive braided yummy egg bread itself that is usually associated with the weekly Sabbath and holy days.

dim (love and kindness), and study in the synagogue replaced the Temple and animal offerings; rabbis who spent years of learning were ordained by their rabbi to lead replaced hereditary *kohanim* (priests); and the age of prophecy or charismatic leadership was declared over. The rabbinic revolution, as I like to call it, was complete.*

Over time, and with the influence of the Islamic empires under which the vast majority of Jews lived and prospered for many centuries (I know this is hard to believe given contemporary reality), the Jewish community developed a system of leadership that divided power between the chief religious leader known as the *Gaon*, and a "secular" political/economic leader known as the *Resh Galuta* who represented them to the powers that be. This was an exact duplicate of the Islamic Empires that divided power in the same way, although at times in the caliphate the power was concentrated in one individual. Rabbinic leadership was local only. At times, the two leaders worked in harmony; but at other times, they were in conflict. And at times they were in conflict over such issues as the calendar with the minority of Jews who lived in the Promised Land then called Palestine. Ashkenazi Jewry (which developed much later than the Sephardic and Mizrachi communities) was further decentralized, with individual rabbis holding much more authority in the religious, political, and economic spheres.

Fast forward two thousand years from the beginning of the Geonic period (or one thousand from its completion), the leadership of the Jewish community, with many more organizations and institutions, is basically still divided in the same way. There are many religious leaders, divided into four primary movements—Reform, Conservative, Reconstructionist,

---

*Hundreds of years earlier, around 570 BCE, the Babylonians conquered Judea and destroyed the first Temple, carrying off all of the leadership and intelligentsia into exile, a type of "house arrest." In the ancient world, when one's House of God was destroyed, the people of that faith took on the faith of the conquerors, for after all, their God defeated your God. Every known people did that. Except for the Jewish people. We had prophets who declared that this was a punishment by our God, that our exile would be temporary, and that we could demonstrate ongoing fidelity to our God outside the Land of Israel, even without our Temple! In other words, contrary to what the Torah said, they innovated or adapted to a new reality. Guess what? Seventy years later, King Cyrus of Persia conquered the Babylonians and encouraged the Jews to return to their land and rebuild their Temple. A minority, led by scribes, returned to do just that and, with Cyrus's financial help, built the second Temple. For his role, Cyrus was called a *mashiach*, an anointed one of God, by the author of the Book of Chronicles. Much later the term "*mashiach*" was styled with a capital *M*, giving birth to Christianity, but this is a topic for another book.

and Orthodox—and political/economic/social leaders with more organizations than any one of us could possibly name. There can be no doubt that the structures we created have immeasurably benefited our people and, in some ways, continue to do so. We are a better, stronger community because of the organizations and institutions we created.

Yet at the same time, we have to realize that the sociological, political, cultural, and economic conditions that gave rise to all of our communal institutions in the late nineteenth and twentieth centuries have radically shifted; some might say they even disappeared altogether. When Jewish doctors could not find residencies, we created the Mount Sinai and Jewish hospital system.* When the country clubs would not admit us as members, we built our own exclusive ones. When our children did not feel comfortable at the Young Men's Christian Association, we founded the Jewish Community Center and the Young Men's Hebrew Association. Today, however, we are welcome everywhere, even pursued, and we find ourselves as members of numerous communities, not just the Jewish one. In fact, for many, as difficult as this is to hear by those leaders who are insiders, the Jewish community is not always primary, and even when it is, it might not always be front and center. Loyalty of all sorts is in decline, and Jews no longer feel compelled to "choose Jewish" for their commitments. They also have no problem moving in and out when other needs take priority. I remember early on in my career calling a parent who failed to reregister her child in our Hebrew school. This was a second-generation family in our synagogue. The parent matter-of-factly told me that her fourth-grade daughter's best friend attended a different synagogue school so they decided to join there. Stunned, I naively asked, "Your daughter is only ten years old and your family has been members here for decades. What happens if they stop being friends?" "Oh," she replied. "We'll probably rejoin." I was stunned. But as I learned over and over again, that is the current reality; institutional loyalty (and not just in the Jewish community) is a thing of the past.

---

*When my wife was pregnant, we sought out an ob-gyn in Milwaukee. Through our connections, we were led to a Jewish doctor whom we loved. We assumed that our baby would be born at Mount Sinai Hospital, so imagine our surprise when he told us that he delivered at St. Mary's. "Why?" we asked. "Because it is the best hospital for obstetrics," he told us rather nonchalantly. And he was the vice president of his Conservative *shul*.

Dr. Gil Rendle, author and longtime lead consultant for the Alban Institute, has written extensively about this topic.[1] He notes that all twentieth-century denominational movements, Christian as well as Jewish, followed pretty much the same pattern, responding to the same needs. They included a need for national, centralized organizational structures; standardized policies and practices; and a chain of command with clear lines of authority and accountability. Today, these are the exact opposite of what is necessary for organizations to thrive.

Everyone agrees on the following set of facts: synagogue membership and attendance are in decline, and while the dollars are still strong, the numbers of donors to major institutions like the United Jewish Appeal federations are fewer and fewer. Additionally, leadership is aging and not being adequately replaced all across the Jewish community (a friend of mine laughs when she says that she received the Young Leadership Award in her community while in her forties), and organizations like B'nai Brith, which brought Jews together for social and philanthropic purposes, are shrinking rapidly. Though no study has been done on this topic, I would wager that only a small minority of the Jewish people truly believe that their prayers are being listened and responded to by a caring God, which might be one factor in shrinking attendance at worship services. After all, that is the structure and premise of the traditional liturgy even now, which is prayed in a language most do not comprehend, with rituals that seem long and boring to most who "attend" as opposed to "participate." In short, we need to ask ourselves the difficult question, "Are the very institutions that were innovations over the past two thousand years now obsolete?" For no matter how well they served us in the past, if they are no longer relevant, we need to allow them to die. We can mourn the loss, but we have to let them go. Remember, the Temple in Jerusalem (with the brief interruption mentioned earlier) lasted almost a thousand years. I am certain at the moment of its destruction many Jews must have felt that Judaism itself was over. But here we are two thousand years later still hanging in there. No structure, no matter how much we love it, is eternal. Just like us.

Though most Jews "pass through a synagogue" at one point or another in their lives, the majority of Jews do not belong to a synagogue today. Why is that? Obviously, many factors contribute, not the least of which are economic, the so-called high price of belonging. But since those same Jews often spend a small fortune on club memberships, vacations, and the like, I think it safe to say that the synagogue is not offering what they want or feel they need; otherwise, they would be there.

Today, most Jews describe themselves as "not religious," or JNRs (Jews of no religion, as Jane Eisner describes it in the September 2018 edition of the *Forward*); hence, there is little need in their lives for organized prayer, especially to a God that they are not sure they believe in, with a prayer book replete with images of hierarchy and kingship that does not speak to them. With the exception of Orthodox *shuls*, which often struggle to get a daily *minyan* (prayer quorum of ten), the vast majority of synagogues have given up on the very idea of three daily worship services and, instead, have adopted the Christian model of once-a-week prayer. Even then, attendance is often sparse, regardless of what rabbis tell you. My personal rule in response to the question "How many people come to synagogue on a 'regular' Shabbat?" is to halve the number of what the rabbi responds. While they still participate in the various life cycle "events," they do so as transitional moments in the lives of only those people they know—their own children, family members, and the children of friends. In other words, they "go" but only when "invited," showing up as late as possible. Their celebration of holidays resembles the family gatherings at Christmas for most Christians, or Thanksgiving for most Americans, not so much as God moments, but as opportunities to be with the people they love and mean the most to them. Not that here is anything wrong with that. Very few adults take advantage of learning opportunities that synagogues and JCCs offer, but they dutifully send their children to suffer Hebrew school like some fraternity rite of hazing—"If I had to go, so do you!" And while Jews do like to attend social events, the synagogue is only one option of many venues now available to them. I would say from my experience, even though this might sound a bit cynical, it depends on the caterer and which of their friends are going more than anything else.

One of the ongoing stories that synagogues sell themselves is that every child needs Hebrew school so that they can become a *Bar/Bat Mitzvah*. They act as if that is some kind of prerequisite for the Jewish family. True, many Jewish adults still value this rite of passage. Others feel that if they had to do it, so do their children—which is not, in and of itself, a terrible motivation. After all, tradition is about passing down to the next generation, even when the reasons for doing so are inchoate. While I have been blessed to study with and officiate with more than a thousand adolescents traversing this important rite of passage, I fully recognize that Hebrew school is often detrimental to a child's well-being and long-term fidelity to the Jewish community. Today's Jewish kids have lots of after-school choices, let alone weekend choices, that are equally if not more valuable to them. Attending Hebrew school often feels punitive. In most communities, we do not have enough dynamic teachers who really turn kids on to Jewish learning. In fact, the number of children who continue studying after the age of thirteen is diminutive. While they happily and proudly celebrated their new status, they saw it as something they "got through" and with which they were now finished and, sadly, will soon forget. Their parents understood it as "a good job" just like their other secular accomplishments. Not exactly a success. Adolescents need a rite of passage that helps them navigate the often murky waters separating child-hood from adulthood, providing them with the "skills" and relationships they will need to become a quality adult. My more than four decades of teaching children have convinced me that around age thirteen is the exact right time because psychologically as well as physically they are truly tran-sitioning from one stage of life to another. Though I fully recognize that having facility with Hebrew is an authenticating Jewish experience, taking four or five years to teach them to merely decode (not read . . . making the right sounds is not really reading . . . if that was the case, I can "read" Greek and Latin!) a language that many of their parents cannot even read may not be the exact challenge that every child needs. It is time to open up the possibilities for what it really means today to be a *Bar Mitzvah* or *Bat Mitzvah* (a true son or daughter of the commandments) and a member of the adult Jewish community, and shut down the typical Hebrew school.

Adding to this decline is the organizational structure called "denomi-nations or movements" of the American Jewish community. While at one point this was a clear identity marker, both religious and sociological, the fact is that most Jews today are not doctrinal so they either feel equally comfortable in any synagogue or are really unaware of denominational differences. All the acronyms feel like alphabet soup, and even our lead-ers cannot decipher them. Most of my board members never knew the difference between the URJ, the CCAR, or the HUC-JIR* despite their

---

*URJ (Union for Reform Judaism); CCAR (Central Conference of American Rabbis); HUC-JIR (Hebrew Union College–Jewish Institute of Religion).

excellent board orientation and handbook. They are more apt to join the synagogue that is closest to their home, or the one with the rabbi they like, or which offers the most flexible or least demanding religious school for their children's busy after-school schedules. And in this day of electronic communication and learning, the synagogue edifice has now become more of a burden that needs supporting than a destination of choice.* On my commute to the synagogue each day during my working years, I passed a number of empty church and synagogue parking lots.

Now the above description may sound harsh and perhaps a bit bitter, but no one doubts the reality of the synagogue's decline, so there must be some reason for it. I know some would like to say it is the high cost of belonging, but there is not a synagogue in the world that does not have a sliding scale for membership. Perhaps people are embarrassed to ask for a discounted membership when they drive up in their Lexus, but such financial support is available and freely given to anyone in need. A full third of the membership in my former synagogue did not pay what we called "fair share dues" and yet were afforded full participation in our community. For decades, sociologists have been documenting the decline of communal organizations.† Perhaps that is the "all of it"? We are merely being caught up in a new sociological reality, and there is little or nothing we can do about it.

I wish I could say what is next or even if there is a next. It took nearly two hundred years for the synagogue to evolve, so the seed of the future might already exist, germinating and getting ready to be born. Or it might not have been created yet. Who knows? What I do know is that experiments like Lab/Shul in New York, or The Well in Detroit, or The

---

*Most people have the mistaken notion that in North America Orthodox Judaism came first, then Conservative, and finally Reform. The truth is the opposite. When German Jews started arriving in North America in the mid-1800s, they brought Reform Judaism with them, and since the traditional Jewish community they found there was both small and unorganized, it grew unabated with little to no resistance. With the arrival of large numbers of traditional Jews from Eastern Europe, the now largely assimilated and successful German Jews wanted to help their brothers and sisters acclimate to America but did not want to be associated with them. Hence, the birth of the Conservative movement! Decades later, as a way to identify who they were, traditional Jews coined the term "Orthodox" (i.e., "right doctrine") distinguishing themselves from both Reform and Conservative Jewry who had, in their opinion, accommodated to America but lost the core of our faith and tradition.

† In *Bowling Alone* (2000), Robert Putnam pointed out that while bowling was more popular than ever, there were, in fact, fewer leagues. Interesting.

Kitchen in San Francisco and others should be encouraged and supported. What I also know is that any institutional structure that automatically assumes unquestioned Jewish loyalty is destined for the dust heap of history. When my father was suffering with Alzheimer's disease, my siblings and I searched for the best possible care for him; we did not automatically go to the Jewish Home, but we did, of course, inquire there. In the end, we chose a nondenominational organization that was incredible. Even now, years after he passed away, we are committed to the place that took such good care of our dad. And if this is my family's experience, all of us strongly identified with the Jewish community, imagine the feelings of those of our tribe who are only marginally connected.

I spent my entire rabbinic career devoted to synagogue life and was actively involved in numerous causes and institutions that worked tirelessly on behalf of our people. I was fortunate to help recreate two dynamic communities that had become moribund, precipitously in decline. I was blessed with many hundreds of volunteers who gave their time and their resources to make our synagogue a place where people would want to spend their time learning, praying, socializing, and working to make the world a better place to be. Yet, despite our success, I also watched as day schools closed, synagogues merged, and organizations struggled and downsized. It is not, nor has it ever been, about the good and important work they sought to do. No one can doubt that their intentions were excellent and their staffs hard working. However—and this is the difficult news that most of us in the Jewish establishment do not want to hear—all of that is basically irrelevant today. There is no automatic loyalty. None. Just because my parents or grandparents belonged to the Workman's Circle (just to name one historically excellent organization) is not enough for me to want to be a part of it or even support it. It has to be personally meaningful to me. Period. End of subject. There are literally thousands of great organizations out there doing great things. As a citizen of the world, which is, let's be honest with ourselves, who we Jews have become, they all have equal access to speak to me. And I am listening.

There is another important factor we must consider. Much, if not most, of the organized Jewish world has operated with the presupposition that those who belong to and/or support them are "settled" in their life situation. That is to say, they are at work in their careers, married, homeowners, and raising children. That reality is simply not aligned with our current millennial generation and, more and more, is not the reality of the baby boomers, either. Our children take longer to figure out what they will be doing with their lives, they marry later, and if they choose to have children at all, they are probably having only one or two. From the time they leave home at age eighteen to go to college (or take that ever more popular gap year to do something amazing) and finally settle down, for the vast majority of them, more than a decade to a decade and a half has passed. In that time, if they have been disconnected from Jewish life (as many have) it is truly challenging to bring them back.

This is why Hillel on college campus becomes so incredibly important. When I went to school, Hillel was the repository of all the Jewish social misfits as well as those seeking a daily *minyan*. Not anymore. Today, Hillel does an incredible job of connecting to our college kids where they are, creating experiences rich in Jewish values that speak to them. Our Hillel at the University of Miami is a cool place to be and is alive with activity. But even that is not enough. After college, most of our children explore for a while, travel, move away from home, go to graduate school, try out a job or two, maybe even go back to school a second or third time. In the mid-2000s, we experimented with an outreach effort aimed at this population. Though it was staffed by one of our rabbis, the funding for what would become known as "Miami Jews" was completely independent. Nevertheless, we had to resist efforts by our Temple to use our ever-growing contact list to solicit membership. That would have been a death knell for sure. What we found is that young adults (both singles and couples), contrary to what is often said about them, are proud of their identity, but they just do not know or have difficulty enunciating specifically what they are most proud of. They want Jewish connection and experiences; they also want to meet Jewish peers in their age demographic. I understand that similar efforts are popping up all over the country, including Hillel International's Base Hillel, for college graduates or Moishe House. This is good. What we have yet to find out is the following: After years of "getting it for free," will this generation be willing to financially support it? For no matter what structures we create, they will not survive (let alone thrive) unless people "step up to the plate," so to speak.

A word about the baby boomers, or empty nesters, as they are often called. Once upon a time, and not so very long ago, to retire meant just that. One stopped work and hung out, sticking close to the adult children and grandchildren, continuing fidelity to the community and organizations that were a part of their working lives. And given life-expectancy statistics, it might not have been a very long period of time. After all, in the early 1900s, only one hundred years ago, the life expectancy for a male was fifty-two years old! All that has changed. There are now periods or decades of retirement. Retirees travel a great deal with many leaving their original home and not necessarily committed to the institutions of their new community, or their former one for that matter. Families are spread out. Many in the grandparent generation choose to attend synagogue at their grandchildren's place, which is where they attend preschool, not necessarily the one where their parents grew up. And this lines up with our younger generation as well; more and more empty nesters are saying, "What's in it for me? The synagogue does not offer me anything." All I am saying here is that the once-reliable pool of retirees committed to the Jewish institutions that were a part of their lives for decades is no longer an automatic. In fact, it is less likely than ever before.

Is the synagogue dead? Not yet. But its health is in real jeopardy. The Renewal movement may yet inject some life into it, just like the Chavurah movement did in the 1980s and 1990s, but it will not be enough to ultimately save it. Are the monoliths of our national organizations dead? The twentieth century saw the growth and development of important organizations that led to the power and prestige of the Jewish community. In this they emulated the Christian as well as the not-for-profit world's organizing principles. For the most part, they were incredibly successful because they were necessary. Success is a funny thing. It too often leads us to want to repeat what we have done in the past well into the future. After all, the thinking goes, it was successful. Why not keep doing it? The operating word here is "was." If the purpose for which an organization was created no longer exists, it will cease to exist. That is a fact of life that cannot be denied. It may die a slow death, with loyalists hanging on for dear life, but it will die. If it has great wealth, or a healthy endowment fund, it can slow down its demise, convincing those who love it that it will survive long into the future. Such are the fictions and fantasies we sell ourselves. We love magical thinking in the Jewish world, unsupported by any data.*

---

*The leadership of two synagogues (one Reform, one Conservative) that were thinking of merging sought my counsel. With a demographic shift, both had been declining in membership for years. They presented their plan to me, which included the sale of one

Only a shift or change in mission combined with an exciting or uplifting vision will ultimately infuse new life into our communal structures.

But mission and vision alone won't do it. The very structure can also be a problem. When I lived in Wisconsin, I used to shop at a small family-run grocery. The people who worked there were friendly and always helpful. They knew all their regular customers. On Sunday mornings, the line for its bakery products was literally out the door. By any measure, it was a huge success, and it was always a pleasure to shop there. Then, the gas station that was adjacent went out of business. The adult children decided this was the right time to expand and so they bought the gas station and built an addition to the grocery, tripling its size. And within a year, it went out of business. Bigger is not always better. The very size of some of our national as well as local organizations is a problem today. Many will have to downsize if they wish to become agile and adaptive, as well as responsive and thus effective in the future.

Further, there are some uncomfortable realities that have to become the subject of fully transparent and open dialogue. There is an old joke that the Jewish community lives by the Golden Rule. That is, the one who has the gold, rules. In almost every Jewish organization, disproportionate power is wielded by wealthy donors. This creates "shadow leadership," which disempowers as well as discourages those who volunteer and are elected to lead. No wonder most Jewish organizations say they have trouble finding volunteers. I have even heard of agreed upon board decisions

---

of their buildings but no noticeable change in staff expenses. "What do you think, Rabbi Bookman?" After a long pause, I responded, "You have both been experiencing significant shortfalls over the past number of years, correct? And the donors, who have been writing the checks to make up the losses are no longer willing to do so, correct?" They answered "yes" to both questions. "Well, since you have no plan to change the expense line, how are you going to make up the difference?" "With new members, of course." "Have either of your synagogues grown in the past five years?" "No, but they will once we merge. And in the meantime, we will use the sale of the building to fill in the gap." I did some quick math and realized that the income from the sale would hold them for two to three years at most. When I pointed this out, they reminded me of the growth spurt they would certainly experience by creating this new and unique interdenominational synagogue. I agreed that the new mission was exciting, but I also pointed out some new organizational challenges they would soon experience and some possible pathways that could help them thrive into the future. In the end, they went ahead without addressing the concerns I raised and, five years later, had to shut down. These two slowly sinking ships merely anchored together, thinking that would help them sail. They only sunk faster.

being erased from the board minutes after the handful of true decision makers met with the professional leadership and "rethought" and overturned them. Not only is this disgraceful, but it is illegal for a nonprofit to do so! Yet, it is regularly and shamefully done. Shame on us!

The organized Jewish community has to recognize that the social realities of the founding generation no longer exist. In the past, belonging to a synagogue and donating one's resources to the Jewish community was an expectation. It was most often a boon to their social as well as professional lives. Unsophisticated (and often undereducated) donors were happy to allow the rabbis and professionals make decisions for them. Today's volunteer is more often than not a well-informed, successful professional with a leadership role in their business life. They have limited time and want to make a real difference. They want to use their gifts and talents so that their volunteer experience will be meaningful. Unfortunately, more often than not, they are frustrated by their experience in the Jewish world, which they find slow, cumbersome, and full of bureaucracy, with their efforts not truly appreciated. With rare exceptions, for this generation, being put on a committee sounds like a life sentence, not an opportunity to make a difference.

And then there is the money. Belonging to the Jewish community is expensive. And not only that, when I make a small donation to a secular organization, I receive immediate gratitude in the form of a letter or e-mail. When I make a donation to the Jewish community, most often I receive a "bill" for the following year with an expected 10 percent increase. To not do so is to be looked upon as some sort of piker, unwilling to step up and do the right thing. Synagogues still charge dues, as if the members actually owed them something. Don't they yet realize that any monies sent to a synagogue are a gift, not an obligation? To make matters worse, too often the first conversation synagogues have with potential members is a financial one—here is what it costs to belong—a total turnoff. It needs to be the other way around. People need to be brought into the community, be touched by it, have an opportunity to experience the best of what it has to offer, and only then be asked to provide support. A confident community, proud of itself and what it has to offer, does just so.

And finally, we have to ask ourselves the painful question, "Do the Jewish people still need us?" I am certain the priests in the ancient Temple in Jerusalem thought that the people could not live without them. After all, they did a Torah-ordained (read commandment or *mitzvah*) function of reconciling people to God. The Temple was no doubt the largest Jewish institution of its time. It inspired awe and obedience for generations, for more than a millennium. The point should be clear. Insiders always think we are indispensable. But history and life should teach us that we are not. Are we living in the generation that history will say was the end of the synagogue/Jewish organization era? Only time will tell. But one thing is certain: unless significant changes are made, the end is not so far into the horizon. Last Jewish organization standing, please turn off the lights.

• 8 •

Israel: Ingathering or Impediment?

The image of the ship *St. Louis* being turned away from American and other world ports has been burnished into the modern consciousness of every concerned Jew. Not only do the faces of those aboard continue to haunt us, and their subsequent murders at the hands of the Nazis plague us, but the very notion of "no place to go" profoundly altered Jewish thinking in the twentieth century. Though it was already in the Zionist air, so to speak, I am certain this episode had a deep impact on the creation of the Law of Return, the single piece of legislation that guarantees any Jew, anywhere, a safe haven upon reaching the Land of Israel. As the poet Robert Frost once wrote, "Home is where, when you have to go there, they have to take you in."[1] The millions of lives this Law of Return has already saved have changed the Jewish landscape forever.

At the same time, it has created a new potential problem. If Israel understands the need for safe haven for its own people, what about other refugees whose lives are at serious peril? Are Jewish lives inherently more valuable than those of other people? As we have seen in recent decades, there are asylum-seeking refugees (or illegal immigrants depending on one's political leanings) from numerous countries (especially war-torn African nations) who now see Israel* as an oasis in the storm.[2] Israel's

---

*It has been alleged that Prime Minister Netanyahu, who calls these refugees "infiltrators" who "pose a real threat to the future of the State of Israel," signed a deal with Rwandan president Paul Kagame to deport them to Rwanda. Human rights groups have universally condemned this action, including the Israeli-based Hotline for Refugees and Migrants. Its spokesperson, Dror Sadot, tweeted, "The entire world is dealing with millions of refugees. It's baseless for Israel, a developed country, to claim that it cannot take

taking in of these people from Eritrea and Sudan, and other such trouble spots, now numbering more than fifty-five thousand, has created a social quagmire—how can these people, most of whom are Muslim, ever integrate into modern Israeli society? Today, they live in poverty in Tel Aviv or in desert camps called *holot*, literally "sands" in Hebrew. Since they are not Jewish, they are not citizens and are denied access to free health care. Their children, many of whom were born in Israel, are not granted Israeli passports and must attend separate schools. Last May, Israel required that 20 percent of asylum seekers' salaries be put into a fund that would be released to them only if they relocate outside of Israel. They thought they were coming to a democratic country to save their lives. Now they wonder; many having given up any hope altogether.

An even "crazier" scenario presented itself while I was meeting with friends in Israel during the summer of 2018. As the Russian- and Iranian-backed Syrian army was squeezing the last remnants of the rebels in the southwest corner of the country, thousands made their way to the border on the Golan Heights. While Israel was quick to make medical treatment readily available in Israeli hospitals, and while it provided tons of humanitarian aid (both admirable seeing as Syria has been a long-term enemy), the government was equally quick to declare that it would not receive a single individual as a refugee into the land of Israel. Now for the crazy part. In interviews with the understandably distraught Syrians at the border, many said they would welcome the opportunity to become full-fledged, law abiding Israeli citizens. I instantly thought to myself, what a public relations coup for Israel to do the right thing here! But not unexpectedly, Israel allowed this opportunity to slip through its fingers. Imagine had it acted with an open heart, remembering our own history of being the wandering refugee outsider? Even if they only accepted a token number of these desperate and unfortunate individuals, what a statement that would have made about who we really are as a people. In Jewish circles, they used to say about the Palestinians, "They never miss an opportunity to miss an opportunity." Perhaps the same can now be said about the Israelis.

I fully understand how difficult this is for Israel. However, it could get even more complicated. What if a number of these refugees had claimed they were Jewish? What if millions of impoverished, underedu-

---

its part in carrying the burden." When the deal was exposed, and international pressure escalated, Rwanda backed out.

cated people all over the world started to lay claim to ancient ancestry as members of the Ten Lost Tribes? What if they started acting and behaving like Jews? Praying in Hebrew? Wearing *tzitzit* (fringes) and *kippot* (*yarmulkas* or skullcaps)? And more important, what if they expressed their desire to return to the Land of Promise under the Law of Return, citing danger to their very existence simply because they were Jews? What would Israel do? This is no longer fiction or some made-up scenario for this chapter of my book.* Eyewitnesses in the latter stages of Ethiopian immigration say that men of various faiths were putting on Jewish garb just to get out of their country. I am certain that was true.

We know with some certainty that not every individual who arrived in the massive wave of Russian immigration in the 1990s was, in fact, Jewish. Yet, for the most part, they were welcomed.† Later on, some wound up leaving the country for Europe, Canada, and the United States; most have stayed. Many live ostensibly Jewish lives today. Others do not. Yet by all accounts, their *alliyah*, more than a million strong, has been a tremendous success, transforming Israeli society as well as its economy. For sure, much of it had to do with the fact that they were well educated and came with marketable twentieth-century skills. But at the same time, we must ask ourselves an uncomfortable question. Did their acceptance and fairly rapid integration into Israeli society have anything to do with the fact that they were white skinned and from a nation whose Jewish population were by and large Ashkenazi?

Let's assume for a fact that *not* everyone (we don't know how many) who has achieved status as an Israeli citizen under the Law of Return was

---

*The Abayudaya of eastern Uganda practice Judaism, keep Shabbat and holy days, and maintain *kashrut* (kosher food) as their diet. Their spiritual leader, Gershom Sizomu, was educated and ordained a rabbi by the Ziegler School of Rabbinic Studies in Los Angeles, California. They are recognized by both Conservative and Reform Judaism as being Jewish. Sadly, in a recent decision, the Knesset refused to recognize this community, which has suffered greatly exactly because of their identity with the Jewish people; their numbers diminished especially under the former dictator Idi Amin.

† In a brand new 2018 exhibit titled *Pravda* (the Russian word for "truth") at the Israel Museum in Jerusalem, artist Zoya Cherkassky exposes for the first time in art some of the uglier sides of this *alliyah*. Through some stunning images, Cherkassky shows that these new immigrants had to deal with humiliation while facing the question of Jewish identity in their meeting with the Jewish rabbinic establishment. Theirs was an Israeli-Zionist ethos, not a religious one. After decades of hoping to leave the former Soviet Union, suffering for their intention to do so, and experiencing numerous hardships for identifying as Jews, they were ill prepared for the arrogance and dismissal of their "interrogators."

really Jewish. Though there are no statistics, I am certain it has happened. But, has it damaged the Jewish character of the State of Israel? Has Israel been able to absorb this tiny drop of "fake Jews" without changing the fabric of the nation? In other words, if the numbers remained small, as it most likely will, is this really a problem? I hardly think so.

Currently, one-fourth of Israeli citizens are not Jewish, and yet Israel is a Jewish state. Even if that number grew to one-third, would it really change anything? Perhaps the time has come for the Law of Return to be amended. Perhaps this life-saving measure in the early days of the State of Israel is no longer absolutely necessary. Perhaps, like other nations, Israel wants to cap or control immigration, though I continue to hear hopes for double or even triple the numbers currently living there, with Be'er Sheva becoming a desert city like Phoenix, Arizona. Perhaps citizenship has to become conditional, dependent on timely acts of Jewish identity (whatever they may be thought to be). In the 1970s and 1980s, there was great concern that Israel's best and brightest were leaving the country. We know of so-called *yoredim* (literally, "those who went down," or left the country, as opposed to those who "went up" by making *alliyah*) all over the world. Just travel to the far reaches of our planet and you will find good falafel restaurants run by Israelis who left their country, as well as academics, engineers, physicians, and Hebrew school teachers.* Or perhaps the time has come for Israel, the historic home of the Jewish people, to embrace the reality of a multicultural society and the gifts that brings to any nation.

It seems to me that Israel's new "problem" is that, despite all the apparent dangers, millions the world over now see Israel as a great place to live, work, and raise a family. After all, most demographic predictions say that Israel will soon surpass the United States containing the largest Jewish population in the world.† That's what we call a "good problem" to

---

*I remember walking out of my hotel in Cusco, Peru, prior to my trek to Machu Picchu. Imagine my surprise when I saw a sign for an Israeli restaurant! Then my gaze traveled across the street where I saw another one, looking almost exactly the same. When I inquired as to the origin of these two restaurants in that close proximity, my host said, "Originally, there was one restaurant opened by two friends who had traveled here after their army service. They had a falling out and one of them opened the identical restaurant across the street. They still don't talk to one another."

† The current debate among Jewish demographers calls into question just how many Jews there are living in the United States, from as low as 5.7 million to as high as 7.1 million. Israel now has more than six million Jews living there. In other words, depend-

have! And perhaps, in a nation in which some three-fourths of its citizens claim to be secular—many of whom prefer the moniker "Israeli"—the time has come to ask ourselves, "What does it really mean to be Jewish or even have a Jewish state?" And more precipitously, "Who gets to decide?" Currently, such issues are left to the "rabbinate," which is totally dominated by ultra-Orthodox and Haredi parties who have much to gain both economically and politically by preserving the status quo. You see, though many drop out of those communities, their birthrate continues to be higher than the national average. Growing the population with secular and liberal Jews, as well as non-Jewish citizens, would serve to dilute their numerical advantage. Keeping Jews out by claiming that they are not really Jewish maintains, and even increases, their power. But this position is plagued by the disease "short-term-itis." As this population tends to not serve in the Israel Defense Forces (IDF), is under- or unemployed (because their separate educational system does not prepare them for the twenty-first-century workforce), and does not pay taxes but receives welfare assistance, the status quo, as most Israelis know and talk about in private, becomes simply unsustainable. (I look at these identity questions in greater depth in chapter 3, titled "Who Is a Jew?")

Though many claim to be descendants of the *b'nai anusim* (those Sephardic Jews who were forced to convert to Christianity in 1492), I insist on full conversion including circumcision or *hatafat dam* for males, immersion in *mikveh* for everyone, and appearance before a *bet din* after a year-long course of study and involvement with the Jewish community. It has been one of the great blessings and privileges of my rabbinate to guide people on their journey to Judaism. Of the close to one thousand people who have converted with me, not one was ever seriously questioned as to his or her identity or faith, either in the United States or in Israel. Until now. Four committed individuals from Latin America have attempted to make *aliyah* under the Law of Return (one of whom was married to

---

ing on whose numbers one believes, either Israel is number one or number two in the world in Jewish population. What all demographers agree upon is the following: Israel's numbers are growing due to a high birthrate and continued immigration; everywhere else, Jewish population is in decline. Interestingly, a slight spike in Jewish population occurred in Germany after the collapse of the Berlin Wall and the relaxation of emigration from Russia. Those numbers have now normalized, with a fair number of ex-pat Israelis living comfortably in Berlin, Frankfurt, and Munich. Of course, like most Israelis living in *chootz l'Aretz* (outside the Land of Israel), they swear it is only "temporary."

a Jewish man born in Israel). All four applications were rejected. All four were educated and self-sufficient. And, all four were racially mixed. What I was told by a representative of the Jewish Agency is that Israel does not want to open a potential floodgate of poor immigrants from Latin America and elsewhere who may not be "really Jewish." He also added that if they truly want to be Jewish they should study with a local rabbi and be part of the Jewish community. When I pointed out there were no local rabbis among the population I was serving, and that the local synagogue will most often not even allow them to attend prayer services, he suggested they go to Argentina to study. Biting my tongue, I replied, "Look at a map! Buenos Aires is not exactly around the corner." By the way, my offer to fly him to Guayaquil, Ecuador, to actually see the alternative community we have created and meet the people so that he could form his own opinion, was rejected. He would rely on the Israeli Consul there, the local wealthy owner of the synagogue whose main goal was to delegitimize those returning to their Jewish roots. This was the same man who instructed the managers of his supermarkets to not sell *matzah* (unleavened bread) before *Pesach* (Passover) to anyone not on his approved list of Jewish Community members! So much for the model of *keruv* (literally, to "bring near") set for us by our ancestors Abraham and Sarah!

There is a widespread feeling in the Jewish world that anti-Israel sentiment is really the new or thinly disguised anti-Semitism. After all, in almost all circles, it is completely not politically correct to admit any anti-Jewish bias in today's world. As a result, Israel becomes a convenient proxy. While this might be true for some of Israel's critics, I do not share that opinion. And I think it is dangerous for us to play the anti-Semitism card in this regard. Nevertheless, I really hate to "pick on" Israel. After all, it is truly remarkable what Israel has accomplished under difficult, if not dire, circumstances. Israel has more nongovernmental organizations (NGOs) per capita than any industrialized nation. When disaster strikes anywhere in the world, its first responders are most often there first, setting the standard of rescue and care for all who follow. Despite decades of violence, many organizations like B'tzelem, Haqel, or Rabbis for Human Rights work tirelessly on behalf of the Palestinian population. And Israel has so many inspiring individuals like Chaim Peri, the founder of the remarkable Yemin Orde Youth Village and its program of *tikkun lev* (repairing), healing the hearts of children who have suffered trauma and loss.

Yet, to those of us the world over who have loved and supported Israel, whose children have made *alliyah* and served in the IDF, who do business in Israel and have even built factories there, who have donated billions of dollars and invested even more, and who, quite frankly, enjoy spending time there, it seems that Israeli society is sliding ever more precipitously into a semi-theocracy in which the vast majority of the population will be held religious hostage by a minority of ultra-Orthodox (*haredim*) who provide little but demand much. These *haredim*, who refuse to serve in the army or do national service and who are a drain on the economy, are at the vanguard of the settler movement who firmly believe that *all* of the West Bank (which they call by their biblical names of Judea and Samaria) should be part of a new, greater Israel. They cavalierly trample on Palestinian rights, use violence and intimidation with relative impunity against the Arab population, are opposed to the two-state solution or any territorial compromise, and have already suggested that voluntary emigration or forced expulsion or even full annexation would be their preference to solve the so-called Arab problem. These *haredim* demand full control of all religious matters, deeming that they, and only they have the religious knowledge and commitment to make decisions on the part of the State of Israel and its citizenry. These *haredim* and their supporters in the Knesset have little patience for the ideals of Western democracy of full equality under the law, mutual respect, and religious pluralism, which are at the core of the State of Israel's founding principles.*

Instead of opening Israel to greater inclusion, these *haredim* are busy finding ways to "de-Jew" vast swaths of our people. With "declining market share," our own people are finding ways to shrink our base. Unbelievable! And though Israel's Supreme Court regularly rules against them, upholding the fundamental equality and the rights of all those who dwell in the Land, these *haredim* and their corrupt political supporters continue to brazenly ignore the law, create legislative loopholes, and act with seemingly relative

---

*Israel's Declaration of Independence emphatically states, "THE STATE OF IS-RAEL will be open for Jewish immigration and for the Ingathering of the Exiles; it will foster the development of the country for the benefit of all its inhabitants; it will be based on freedom, justice and peace as envisaged by the prophets of Israel; it will ensure complete equality of social and political rights to all its inhabitants irrespective of religion, race or sex; it will guarantee freedom of religion, conscience, language, education and culture; it will safeguard the Holy Places of all religions; and it will be faithful to the principles of the Charter of the United Nations."

impunity backed by a Knesset (and at times the police or army), which often turns a blind eye to their trampling on the law of the Land and the spirit of our faith. While there can be no doubt that Israel is the only true democracy in the Middle East, at the same time we have to own up to the fact that it has yet to live up to its own declared vision.

We in the United States understand that the separation of church and state is for the health and well-being of both, and the only way to guarantee there will be no religious coercion. The state, composed of citizens from many faith traditions as well as secular ones, needs to govern, divorced from religious dogma or controls in order to remain just. Religions, founded in faith, need to remain voluntary commitments devoid of all compulsion or pressure. That is the only way faith commitments can be intellectually honest and spiritually pure. However, throughout its almost seventy years of history, Israel's parliamentary system, which needs a coalition of parties in order to govern, has given outsized power to this ultra-Orthodox minority. With the rare exception of a unity government, like the one Yitzhak Rabin courageously formed leading to years of flourishing and worldwide positive acclaim (but at the same time got him assassinated by a disciple of one of these fundamentalist rabbis), both leading parties from the Left and the Right have sold the souls they don't believe in, in order to attain their voting bloc in the Knesset.* This has led to widespread corruption and ensuing apathy in the political as well as the social, religious, and economic spheres.

This was made eminently obvious in the recent decisions to halt Natan Sharansky's carefully brokered creation of the egalitarian section at the Western Wall and to turn all conversions over to the established Orthodox rabbinic courts. This latter decision got so much worldwide negative pushback that Prime Minister Netanyahu put a six-month halt in order to study the issue further. In doing so, Israel, spearheaded by the likes of minister of culture Miri Regev—who recently told liberal Jews in Argentina not to come to our Homeland unless they plan to practice Orthodoxy—marginalized and delegitimized 90 percent of

---

*I do not include their names because I do not wish to give them any more notice or notoriety than they already have attained. This follows a long-standing Jewish tradition of *y'mach sh'mo* (may his name be erased) when hearing the name of someone who has seriously caused damage to our people.

world Jewry.[3] Or, as Orthodox rabbi Seth Farber writes in the *New York Times* on August 1, 2018,

> I have not been detained by the Israeli police on my way to morning prayers, but I am preparing for that eventuality. That's the new reality of life in the Jewish state for those of us who publicly oppose Jewish fundamentalism. Just ask my colleague Rabbi Dov Hayoun. On July 20, Rabbi Hayoun, a prominent Conservative rabbi, was awakened at 5:30 a.m. by the police at his home in Haifa and taken to a station for questioning. What was his alleged crime? Performing a Jewish wedding in the Jewish state. . . . The potential punishment: two years in prison.[4]

You see, in Israel only the ultra-Orthodox chief rabbinate is responsible for sanctioning all Jewish weddings and divorces. Rabbi Hayoun, like hundreds of other rabbis, is not on the approved list, and neither are any liberal rabbis. Increasingly, modern Orthodox rabbis are not on the list either. It remains to be seen what long-lasting impact that will have on support for Israel in the Diaspora. But with such support already in serious decline among those in the under forty set, Gen Xers, millennials, and the like, this is an extremely dangerous game for Israel to be playing. Perhaps Prime Minister Netanyahu thinks Israel no longer needs American Jewry, as he courts the fundamentalist Christian Right and other conservatives.* Perhaps he believes that he has a "pro-Israel" ally in President Trump whose publicity stunt of moving the U.S. embassy to Jerusalem played well to his base but fooled no one there. In point of fact, the actual embassy and all its activity is still in Tel Aviv while the consulate building in Jerusalem remains empty most days, despite the hokey plaque in front. However, presently Israel runs the risk of disenfranchising world Jewry at a time when Israel's true friends can be counted on one hand. Not smart.

---

*I was flipping channels one night on a recent trip to Israel, and I saw this "hawker" holding a *shofar* (ram's horn) like a prop. He was paraphrasing a biblical passage that declares, "As we bless Israel, God will bless us," and then he said, "So send us your $1,000 pledge to Day Star." Just then a video of Prime Minister Netanyahu speaking to the United Nations regarding Israel's great economic success in multiple fields of endeavor appeared on the screen. I nearly became ill as I thought to myself, "Are these Israel's new friends?"

In his op-ed piece, "The Fracturing of the Jewish People," William Galston uses the image of red states and blue states to make the point that we are rapidly slipping into an insurmountable divide between the two largest Jewish communities in the world—Israel and the United States. He writes,

> In effect, Israeli Jews are a red state while American Jews are a blue state. Seventy-seven percent of Israeli Jews approve of President Trump's handling of relations between the U.S. and Israel, compared with only 34% of American Jews. Eighty-five percent of Israeli Jews, but only 46% of American Jews, back Mr. Trump's decision to recognize Jerusalem as Israel's capital and move the embassy there. Fifty-nine percent of American Jews support dismantling at least some settlements . . . only 39% of Israelis would do so. Eighty percent of American Jews but only 49% of Israeli Jews favor allowing Reform and Conservative rabbis to officiate at Israeli weddings, divorces and conversions. And 73% of American Jews but only 42% of Israeli Jews support both sexes praying together at the Western Wall rather than the strict separation required by Orthodox Judaism.[5]

Galston concludes that when Israel acts as the guardian of the patrimony of the entire Jewish people, it has a greater responsibility to weigh the views of the entire worldwide community. This is what is at stake as Israel drifts toward an ultranationalist state, courting the so-called V-4 nations especially Hungary, condemning liberal NGOs, and allowing firms like Black Cube to undermine elections around the world through the blatant misuse of social media. Are we heading toward a new contemporary reality—two Jewish peoples? I hope not. But as any student of Jewish history can tell you, such rifts have taken place in our people's history and never have they served us well.*

At the same time, if one thinks that in this current global economy and interdependence that Israel can go it alone, let me point to the other nation who thought that was possible only a couple of decades ago in the 1990s—South Africa. It was not the pressure of other African na-

---

*The Northern Kingdom and the Southern Kingdom, Pharisees and Saducees, Babylonia and Palestine, Rabbinites and Karaites, and Hasidim and Mitnagdim are examples. At times these were merely ideological splits; at other times, they were marked by the use of *herem* (excommunication) or even outright physical violence.

tions that ultimately brought about the revolutionary change that ended apartheid and brought Nelson Mandela to power. The African National Congress as well as other groups organized local boycotts of the bus system, beginning in Alexandra in 1957. The cultural and academic boycott movement soon followed. But in the end, it was the "white-skinned world," spearheaded by the British as well as the United Nations, that united against South Africa and forced it to change. It is no mere coincidence that the U.S. civil rights movement learned from this example organizing bus boycotts in the South. Israel ought not risk being smug in saying it won't happen to us. It can. This is not to suggest that Israel practices apartheid—far from it. Any suggestion to the contrary is pernicious and totally unjustified by the facts on the ground. Nevertheless, the comparison of a successful but isolated nation, speaking a language that no one else speaks, whose politically and economically dominant population arrived from Europe only a short time ago, and which is regularly opposed in the United Nations by the vast majority of the world's nations, is both startling and apt. In fact, there is already an active worldwide Boycott Divest Sanctions (BDS) movement, with calls from within Israel to end all business relationships with any company profiting from the territories. Only bringing Israel to its economic knees, the argument goes, will force a change. I have heard it said that the Netanyahu government fears BDS even more than it fears a nuclear Iran. I understand why. While I am not a big proponent of economic boycotts, after all, our people have been the victims of such actions throughout our history, one has to admit they are often quite effective. In fact, because the economy is booming both in Israel and the West Bank, there is a sense of satisfaction and apathy toward the "situation" as it is now regularly called. Though I know the following statement will be disputed, in a real way, both the Israelis and the Palestinian leadership on the West Bank (not Gaza) are benefiting from the current status quo. This is why there is little to no energy to make a change. All it would take right now is a small shift in U.S. policy, or a return to the policy in the early years of the State of Israel to tip the balance. Dare we forget the lessons of history?*

---

*In 1956, when Israel took over the Suez Canal with the help of Great Britain and France, it was the United States that pressured Israel to withdraw, which it felt forced to do. Even during the Six Day War, the United States was reluctant to come to Israel's military aid, requiring Israel to turn to both France and South Africa to resupply its military

But perhaps even more important, it is time for Israelis (for ultimately this is their decision, not ours) to ask themselves what will be the character and nature of this Jewish state. Will it even be the Jewish state, or will it slide into being a state for Jews? Will it live up to its promise and become the true nation of *all* Jews everywhere, the Jewish Homeland? Or will it become the domain of that arrogant few who, with God (and politicians) on their side, would impose their will upon us all? The former is what most of us have spent decades hoping and praying and working for; a big vision expectation of a fully inclusive Israel, guided by Jewish values, with freedom of self-expression for all of its citizens. An Israel that makes us proud just as it has for much of its history. An Israel that is truly a light unto the nations. A thriving Israel that empowers world Jewry to thrive. Not a perfect place; there is no perfection in this world. But our place. *All* of ours. Or will it be the latter, exclusionary, tribal, and inherently undemocratic, which would turn both the majority of Jews and others off, and away? I have no doubt that such a path would lead to our decline as a people.

As of 2018, it appears that Israel (emboldened by the U.S. president, along with other reactionary governments around the world) has chosen the latter route, as the new controversial "National Home" law indicates.*

---

with much-needed parts. It was only after 1967 that U.S. policy began to shift decidedly toward the Jewish state. The American Jewish community has short-term history-itis and either has forgotten or does not want to face the facts. There is no guarantee of U.S. support, nor should there be. Just like every other nation in the world, the United States has to act in its best interest as determined by its people and their leadership. Or as I said in a sermon not so long ago, "We Jews like to forget that Barack Obama is the president of the United States of America, not the prime minister of Israel." President Obama was often vilified by the right wing as well as many leaders in the Jewish establishment as being not sufficiently supportive of Israel, though U.S. policy did not change one iota during his term of office. I wonder why. Those same people, whose Jewish identity is primarily wrapped up in Israel, tend to give President Trump a pass. But Mr. Trump's so-called pro-Israel credentials obfuscate his alignment with anti-Semitic groups that call for Israel's and the Jewish people's destruction. Once again, this is short sighted and dangerous for Israel—indeed, for all of us.

*The National Home Law, passed just before the Knesset's summer recess in 2018 by a vote of 62–55 (with two abstentions and one member absent) omits any mention of democracy or enunciation of the principle of equality enshrined in Israel's foundational document, its "Declaration of Independence." Additionally, it downgrades Arabic from an official language of the state to one with "special status." Though the bill is largely symbolic, it reflects an attitude that marginalizes its non-Jewish population as well as religious voices that are not Orthodox. And it threatens to undermine support for Israel in the Diaspora. Not surprisingly, all thirteen Arab Knesset members tore up the bill upon its passage, crying out, "Apartheid, apartheid!" And it is not just the National Home Law. In summer 2018,

That is to say, though most of the people who lead the government are not truly religious themselves, it is no accident that they have aligned themselves with the religious Right. Both want to turn back the clock to a premodern reality. Ultranationalists favor "strong man" leadership with a weakening of the power of the courts; the religious Right is most often led by a single charismatic figure, alive or dead. Ultranationalists are anti-democratic and seek to shrink or even eliminate individual human rights; the religious Right is completely nondemocratic and understands the individual as completely subjected to the will of God as interpreted by the leader. Both are anti–free media and anti-science; they have an "us against them" mentality, even as they seek to limit women's voices and roles in the world. Both are anti-abortion. In addition, the religious Right is organized by tightly controlling the community, including their members' access to the outside world, access to education as well as social media, and access to anyone who is not part of their worldview. In other words, it is a closed sociological reality that completely seeks to control its members' thoughts and actions. Pluralism is an alien, even hostile concept as there is only one Truth in the world, and they just happen to have it. This is the clear and present danger that faces Israel if it continues on its present course.

As is often the case, extremist thinking gives rise to the opposite extreme. In fact, what was once thought to be strictly *verboten*, the very question of Zionism has been challenged, not by some anti-Semites disguised as left-wing intellectuals but by Israelis themselves. In a recent op-ed piece in the newspaper *Ha'aretz*, titled "One State, One Vote," Gideon Levy suggested that Zionism equals ideological totalitarianism, in that no one has been allowed to question its legitimacy, neither from the political Right or Left. As a result, Israel has become infected with ultranationalism tainted by racism, which has led to policies that are cruel, discriminatory, oppressive, and disinheriting.[6] It is a testament to the strength of Israel's democracy that such conversations can take place—there. But in the Diaspora, such criticism of Israel would be seen as anathema, with the critics being labeled as self-hating Jews or (somewhat ironically) anti-Semites. I know. I was the recipient of such epithets when I dared preach a sermon

---

the new Boycott Law (meant to combat the BDS movement) was used to bar American journalist and critic Peter Beinart (there for a relative's *Bar Mitzvah*) and master's degree candidate Lara Algassem from entering the country. Fortunately, worldwide public outcry reversed both decisions, but Israel still got a black eye in the process.

in favor of the two-state solution back in the early 1990s. I am certain this chauvinistic attitude led to the exclusion of J Street from the Conference of Presidents of Major Jewish Organizations in 2014. Nevertheless, such action is short-sighted as these conversations will take place either at the *big* table of inclusion, or the other tables where there will be no helpful exchange of ideas. Nationalism was a nineteenth-century concept. The Jewish people, led by the most unlikely hero Theodor Herzl, applied it to our people. The early Zionists believed that Israel could join the community of nations by being both Jewish and democratic. Not all ideas are eternal. And as we evolve, every idea ought to be subject to review, emendation, or elimination. The ability to have such respectful conversations is a sign of strength and needs to be embraced if we are to truly thrive. Is being both Jewish and democratic a pipedream? I sincerely hope not.

And finally, there is the issue that will just not go away—the Palestinians. While I have little doubt that most of the Arab nations could not care less about the fate of these brothers and sisters—yet conveniently use them to leverage anti-Israel sentiment and promote proxy wars—the facts on the ground remain the same. Since its near miraculous victory in the Six Day War, whatever one calls it, Israel controls the fate and political as well as economic destiny of its Palestinian minority. We all know the trope. According to Daniel Bar-Tal, professor emeritus of education at Tel Aviv University, there is a need on the part of all occupiers to build a hegemonic narrative in order to delegitimize and even dehumanize the occupied in order to carry on or justify the occupation.[7] One questions it at one's peril. It might go something like this: *The whole world is against us. Jews only suffered throughout their long experience in the Diaspora. The land of Israel is the only state that ensures our survival. Israel is surrounded by hostile Arab nations that do not and will never accept the presence of a Jewish state in the region. The Palestinian people do not want peace. The Palestinian leadership is not prepared to make significant compromises and has missed every opportunity to reach agreement. Therefore, given the nature and character of the Arabs, we should refrain from any move that entails danger or uncertainty, including the advancement of the peace process. In the face of the threat and danger, maintaining personal and collective security trumps keeping moral and democratic values that* they *do not share anyway.*

Sound familiar? We have heard it, had it shoved down our throats, too many times to count. Israel's operating belief, since the days of Menachem Begin and Moshe Arens is that they can "manage the situation" (as they liked to call it) through force. After all, Israel has most, if not all, of the power when it comes to the Palestinians. They pose no existential threat. However, as we can all validate, the use of force only motivates or controls people's bodies. Hearts and minds can never be won through force. It will take a change in both intellect and spirit to change the facts on the ground. And the major "fact" is the almost unabated expansion of "settlements" in land captured during the Six Day War. Call them what you will, call it "Judea and Samaria," the "West Bank," or "Palestine," the land we are discussing presents a disjointed, noncontiguous, ungovernable mish-mash that no Palestinian leader could accept as a future homeland. Without major adjustments or land swaps, there can be no Palestinian state, and this says nothing about the other intractable issues of Jerusalem as the capital of both peoples, as well as the right of return for Palestinians, which appears to be a nonstarter.

To date, Israel has decided that "occupation" of these people is the lesser of all evils. Withstanding the occasional uprising of violence, or Intifada, while terrifying in some respect, is still preferable to having a sworn enemy literally right on its borders, as is the case with Gaza. Or so the reasoning goes. However, this stalemate has now lasted more than fifty years! An entire generation has known no other reality. And it has come at tremendous cost in human lives, financial resources, and the psyche of two peoples. Though anyone who cares for the safety and security of the Jewish people recognizes the danger in doing so, Israel can only be both a democratic and Jewish state by allowing the creation of a separate Palestinian state in what most of the world calls the West Bank and Gaza. The vast majority of the world, including most of Diaspora Jewry,* believes this is the only equitable solution.[8] Further delays only increase the

---

*Every poll taken in the United States shows that the vast majority of American Jews—as high as 78 percent in J Street's 2018 survey (*The 2018 Jewish Vote: National Post-Election Survey*, November 2018, https://jstreet.org/wp-content/uploads/2018/11/J-Street-2018-Election-Night-Survey-Presentation-110818.pdf)—supports the two-state solution. And though we hear that Israelis think it "dead," more than two-thirds of Israelis continue to support the idea of two separate states, as that is the best (not perfect) opportunity for Israel to remain both a Jewish state and a democracy. The alternative, to annex the territories without full rights for its citizens would be tantamount to real apartheid, a dangerous and slippery slope indeed. Jewish groups like "IfNotNow," while small in number, are beginning to push the boundary and immediacy of this conversation. There will be others if no progress is made.

sense of disenfranchisement from Israel so strongly felt among young Jews today. Blaming the other side for not being a true partner rings hollow in their ears. It does for young, educated Palestinians as well, who more and more are advocating for one state with full inclusion and citizenship in Israel. Though it risks losing the Jewish majority, perhaps the time has come for that possibility to be taken seriously. For no matter what, the problem will not miraculously disappear, and time is not on our side.

Of course, with Gaza the story is somewhat different. There, an entrenched Hamas leadership, locked into a faulty and failed ideology—the Zionists are invaders that must be defeated and crushed, purged from the Land, from the River to the Sea—presents a thornier problem. Until both sides admit the right to secure existence and safe borders, there will be no movement whatsoever with unabated suffering on the part of the local population living in the refugee camps built for them by the Egyptians when they controlled the Strip. Again, Israel has most of the power and largely controls their destiny. A breakthrough can only emerge when the current story each side tells about the other is delegitimized and abandoned. Sadly, I am not optimistic that will happen anytime soon.

There have been several moments in history in which divisions within the Jewish community led to our near demise. The rabbis said that *sinat achim* (the hatred of one Jew of another) was the immediate cause of the destruction of the Temple in the year 70 CE. The subsequent exile and dispersion of our people with all its incumbent suffering for nearly two thousand years was the direct result. The time is now for all well-meaning Jews to unite and demand that Israel live up to its promise. Our blanket, knee jerk, automatic support is no longer tenable, and all signs indicate that even among the most committed it will not continue. Recently, an American philanthropist, Ike Fisher, who is a member of the board of the American Israel Public Affairs Committee (Israel's most powerful lobby in the United States), "suspended" his financial support of Israel to send a wake-up call to its leadership. The government of Israel, says Fisher, "treats with disdain the larger *am Yisrael* [People of Israel]; it lacks the vision that the government represents the entire Jewish world."[9] Such public criticism is rather unprecedented from this level of Diaspora leadership.*

---

*It continues to run "hot" in light of the two decisions mentioned earlier. It seems to many of us in the Diaspora, including such stalwarts like Dennis Ross and Stuart Eizenstat, that Netanyahu is banking on the support of the Evangelical Right who carry more

I will never stop loving Israel. My commitment is unshakable. The land and its people are inexorably linked to my very being. I have lived there on three separate occasions and have visited more times than I can count. Two of my sons made *alliyah* and served in elite combat units of the IDF. I fully appreciate that only Israelis get to vote on these issues. After all, it is their lives—their blood—on the line. Nevertheless, support comes with a voice, not silence. However, support ought not equal blanket approval for anyone or any cause; it never has, and it never will. Because I love this tiny nation, I expect its best in return. We all should. In fact, the thriving of the worldwide Jewish community is, in large part, dependent upon it.

---

clout, especially with President Trump, than the largely liberal American Jewish establishment. And it is true that what was once an enormous addition to the Israeli economy—American Jewish philanthropy—is today only a small drop in an ever-expanding bucket.

· 9 ·

An Open Door:
The "New" Jewish Community

$\mathcal{I}$t was one of our first consulting assignments. After their rabbi had retired, a synagogue asked us to help them reexamine their mission and vision. Upon arrival to the building, we could see no visible way to enter, nor were there any signs providing directions. After circling the building twice, we finally saw someone in the backyard, and he told us where to enter. Sure enough, in an alcove there was an open door. We walked through a very dark hallway, through what we thought might have been their chapel, and only then into a large room where some very friendly people were awaiting our arrival. We laughingly told them we had a difficult time finding the entrance to which they assured us, "Everyone knows how to enter our building." We replied, "Everyone who is already a member." They bristled a bit at our response, but we turned it into a metaphor for our work together—an open door that no one can find— and it has remained in my mind as an apt metaphor for the worldwide Jewish community.

Insiders and outsiders. For those of us on the inside, and I spent more than half my life serving and being one of them, the Jewish community feels like a second home. We know the language and all the acronyms, lots of acronyms. We know the melodies and can fake the words when we have to; we know the rituals, even when to stand and when to sit. We feel the support when we are in need, and we feel the genuine love when we have occasion to celebrate. We participate with (some) regularity, and we volunteer our time and donate our money. We may get angry or frustrated from time to time, think about dropping out altogether, but in the end, we know we won't. In short, we insiders know how to find the door. We feel welcome.

For those on the outside, including (surprise, surprise) many of our children who grew up on the inside, it is just the opposite.* The space feels alien and foreboding. Everyone seems comfortable except them. There is a language that they cannot seem to access, and they don't want to appear stupid (after all, they are quite accomplished in their fields of everyday endeavor), so they don't ask, not even what page we are on. The same goes for the rituals, including when to really show up for the meeting or the service. They think (but never say aloud), "These are the last people I would ask to attend my *simcha* or sorrow; why can't I just be with my family and friends?" Speaking of their friends, none of them are here, and they are uncertain, even if they were here, whether they would all feel a sense of welcome. They do volunteer their time to causes they find personally meaningful, and they donate small amounts of money, usually online (for which they are instantly thanked). But they usually do so through work, or to support a friend in a 5K or a marathon, to causes that feel more universal. "Inside" feels kind of boring and long, and the *shiksa* (though literally, "a non-Jewish woman," it really is a pejorative way of speaking about Gentiles; the masculine *shaygitz* is equally negative in tone) joke they just heard feels really offensive and off-putting because their best friend who is a great person just happens to be a Hindu woman, doing her best to raise Jewish children. They cannot wait to get out of there, if only they could find the door.

I know it is difficult for insiders to hear the latter, but I am sure they nodded their heads, even smiled with the former. But hear it they must if we are truly going to thrive.

Today, we need to ask ourselves some very serious and difficult questions. Are we creating the community that has the willingness and capacity to really make known its location and truly open the door for everyone? My use of the present tense "creating" means this is an ongoing process,

---

*This is an illustration that I am sure is happening all across the Jewish world. My partner has two single daughters who have returned to live in Miami. Though they were brought up in this community, attended day school, traveled to Israel, always belonged to a synagogue, and their mother is a highly visible, active leader in the community, not one Jewish organization or its leadership has reached out to either one of them to invite them to a program, an event, or a gathering! Really, it is shameful for what it says about who we are.

not something that was done once upon a time and is completed. Or, have we become so insular—self-satisfied on the one hand and insecure, fearful, and even xenophobic on the other—that we have no room for anyone who does not "look" like us? In other words, after more than two thousand years of exile and persecution, years in which we became the world's experts at survival and maintaining our culture and traditions, what is the nature and character of the organized Jewish community today? And if what we have is so good, why is it shrinking almost everywhere in the world? If the Jewish community was a business, and our product was committed Jews, it would be incumbent upon us to ask, "Why do we keep losing market share?" Then we would have to figure out a way to fix it if we wanted to stay in business.

One of the exciting innovations in contemporary North America is an organization called Slingshot. This creative group mobilizes young Jewish philanthropists as funders and active change agents who, along with their partners, shape the Jewish community to be vibrant and continuously evolving. Their response to the earlier question is as follows: *The younger generation is not finding a meaningful place in Jewish life. This is happening because the Jewish community isn't doing enough to envision new models of Jewish life and to engage the next generation in shaping the Jewish future.*

I know this from my own experience as well. In 2005, I was asked to interview for the leadership position of a major Jewish organization. Looking around the rather full table of men and women who had given so much of their personal time and resources to build this organization into an international powerhouse, I noticed that I was probably the youngest person there (and I was no longer "young"). So many of their questions were about building the future and getting the younger generation involved, to carry on the work they had started and/or continued. So when it was my time to ask a question, I took a deep breath and said, "Every one of you has certainly earned the right to be at this table. You have individually and collectively given an unbelievable amount of yourselves to shape and maintain this great organization. At the same time, when I look around the room, I cannot help but notice that none of your children are here, yet we have spent a good deal of this conversation talking about them. So, as our kids would say, what's up with that?" After a short pause that felt like an eternity, one woman broke the awkward silence by saying,

"We know what's best for our children, Rabbi!" I knew then I had lost any chance of being considered for the position. I also knew that I had put my finger squarely on the problem.

When I was serving Temple Beth Am in Miami, we hired a consultant to help us rebrand our synagogue's image. We had a long-standing community-wide reputation as being the large and snooty congregation, which did not fit at all with how we saw ourselves. One of the things I clearly remember is being asked, "When someone looks at your website, for that is the current way people first check you out, will they see themselves there? For if they don't, you have already lost them!" That stopped me in my tracks, which I guess was the point. In doing the research for my last book, *This House We Build*, we found that a majority of congregations describe themselves on their websites as "warm and welcoming." Yet when people go there to see how it feels, they are pained that not one person came up to them to even say "hello" or "Shabbat shalom," let alone invite them to their home for dinner.[1] Our practical experience and the myriad horror stories we have heard teaches us that while the leadership might feel that way, newcomers often do not feel welcomed. In fact, many feel the opposite—that not one person among the regulars could care less that they are even there. Most Jewish organizations are filled with good people who truly do not understand why "no one wants to sign up for committees or volunteer anymore. We used to get hundreds of people out to this event. This year we had to cancel it!" Yet when newcomers call or e-mail, they often do not even get a reply. Or if they by some chance just show up, it feels like everyone knows everyone else except them. And if they are bold enough to join, they are often placed on the committee no one wants to be a part of, being told the great lie of Jewish volunteerism, "It won't take up too much of your time!" So to rephrase, if the collective worldwide Jewish community had a website, who would see themselves there? And just as important, who would not?

I am reminded of a true story. A woman who had converted with me years earlier was doing her best to create a Jewish home and raise Jewish children. Shabbat had become an important part of their lives, and rarely did a Friday pass without candles, fresh-baked *challah* on the table, grape juice for the *Kiddush* (sanctification prayer), and a blessing for each of their kids. She also regularly baked a *challah* for her Christian neighbor, and the two families shared one another's holidays. After years of being encouraged by her mother-in-law, she finally worked up the courage to enroll her youngest son in the Mommy and Me class at the local Jewish Community Center (JCC). They went to the information desk to find out where to sign up, and the first question they were asked was, "Are you Jewish?" Needless to say, she left in tears. Both she and her son are blond and blue eyed.

I am certain the JCC staff member meant no harm. I am sure she is a good person filled with good intentions. But her question underlies a certain mentality, or mind-set, which limits us as a Jewish community. Seriously, we need to do some introspection and figure out if we are projecting an image that says singles; single parents; young adults; people of color; members of the lesbian, bisexual, gay, transgender, and queer community; racially mixed families; children who have been adopted from various nations around the world; Jews by Choice; spiritual seekers born to other faiths; special needs individuals; couples who choose to remain childless, and those with limited means need not apply. That's a long list! Certainly, we want to maintain the Jewish integrity of all our institutions. After all, there is still a "J" in the JCC. In an earlier chapter, I questioned whether these institutions have the ability to adapt to our present-day sociological reality to remain viable. Here, I want to ask a more subtle question. How does the reality, the very existence of these institutions, define and in important ways limit the community we have created? In other words, has being Jewish become synonymous with belonging and participating in the institutional structures we created? Where do they go if they do not choose to "belong"?

To be sure, the Jewish community is not a monolith. As the old joke goes, ask ten Jews to describe who we are, and we will have at least twenty opinions! So let me add a twenty-first. While there will be many individuals who will not fall neatly into the following description, I think we will recognize our collective self in this portrait of "us."

The established Jewish community is successful, accomplished, well educated, and probably the wealthiest Jewish community in the history of our people. While Jewish identity remains important, we have largely assimilated into our host cultures. Most of us in the Diaspora would self-describe as "American Jews," not Jewish Americans. The same is true for European, Canadian, Latin American, and Australian Jews as well—nationality comes first. While we have a high retention rate with a very low percentage of Jews actually converting out of Judaism to another religion, if we are honest with ourselves, very few of us would be willing to make any significant sacrifice (beyond a financial one) for our faith or our people. In our modes of dress, language, leisure time, close companions, decor of our homes, choice of occupation, books we read, and music to which we listen, we would find little difference between ourselves and our Gentile neighbors. That is to say, if an alien landed on our planet and followed the average Jewish person around for a normal day, this ET would see almost no difference between the behavior and dress of the Jewish person and any other citizen of that nation.

We are quick to say Jewish values are important to us and tend to think of ourselves as basically good people, but when pushed, many cannot say to which specific Jewish values they ascribe. Instead, they get all generic and mushy as to the source of what they hold to be most sacred. We are generous (both in time and resources) and quite philanthropic, but more and more our *tzedakah* (which we too often mistakenly call "charity") understandably includes many causes not connected to Judaism, especially universities, museums, the arts, and hospitals; after all, we are good citizens, fully participatory in our national cultures. If you don't believe me, just take a look at the donor wall at any of these secular institutions the next time you are there and notice the high percentage of identifiably Jewish names.

We complain that it costs a lot to be Jewish, but we do pay the price. (However, more and more of our children are opting out, or seeking free opportunities to participate. I mean, just to cite one example, how many would have gone on a Birthright trip to Israel if they had to pay for it? The founders and funders of that great project understood the reality. They truly got it. Very few would say "no" to a free trip!) We are well read but not necessarily when it comes to classical Jewish texts or Jewish history. I doubt most Jews could even name the five books of the Torah in Hebrew or English. In other words, we know a lot more about wine, art, and music than the Talmud, or what really happened to our people in medieval times, let alone ancient times, or the difference between what it meant to be a Jew living in the Christian world versus the Arab/Muslim world. While some of us can read Hebrew, very few of us actually understand the words, and even fewer speak the language (with the exception of Israelis, of course). While we dutifully make the pilgrimage to attend worship services on the High Holy Days as well as life cycle events (but only when invited), most of us are fairly secular in our behavioral and belief patterns. Religious denomination and fidelity used to mean a lot, but today, since we really do not know the true differences between them (we think Orthodox is more, Conservative is medium, Reform is less, and Reconstructionist, what is that?) most of us comfortably attend services and programs that interest us at any synagogue. For example, I used to have a number of people come to my Torah study session on Shabbat mornings and then with no ambivalence go *daven* (pray) at their Orthodox or Conservative synagogue. At the same time, many of us still feel uncomfortable in a church worship service.

While most Jews have close friends, even family, who come from other faith traditions, still we tend to primarily associate with other "members of the tribe." While we may not be happy about it, for the most part we have accepted that our children will intermarry, yet almost none of us are willing to lose them or our future grandchildren over it. The days of "sitting *shivah*" over that choice are truly over. Jews are for the most part liberal, or at least lean that way especially when it comes to social causes, though the percentage of conservatives—especially when it comes to economic issues—has grown in the last couple of decades. We are supportive of Israel, yet astonishingly, a majority of us have never been there. Very few of us have actually experienced acts of anti-Semitism, but still we are concerned about it. We take pride in the accomplishments of other Jews and are embarrassed, even ashamed, when Jews commit some wrongdoing, especially when it makes the news. And though we might no longer admit to doing so, many of us still check the news for Jewish names when some disaster strikes. I would not call us smug, but we tend to be fairly confident and comfortable in who we are and what we have accomplished. We are overwhelmingly Ashkenazi and "white" with little to no understanding of Sephardic or Mizrachi culture. And though some of us still remember grandparents who came as immigrants or refugees, more and more we are far removed from that newcomer experience.*

*One notable exception might be the fairly large number of Ashkenazi Jews from Latin America who have immigrated to the United States and Canada, escaping political persecution and economic instability in their native countries. I was blessed with many members of these communities when I served a pulpit in Miami. In Latin America, the tendency was to create well-organized, coherent communities that were somewhat removed from their host culture, though part of the reason for that is sociological and economic rather

I fully realize not everyone will agree with this description, and some will even resent it as overly negative. I present it here with no judgments attached. Unless we are willing to take an honest look in the mirror, there can be no possibility of transformation or change. That is true both on the personal as well as the communal level. But even if my group portrait is not 100 percent accurate, I do think we can agree that we are recognizable in my words, especially those of us who live in the largest Diaspora community of North America. Obviously, I left out the Orthodox communities because, first, outside of Israel, their numbers are negligible when it comes to the community as a whole (currently less than 10 percent) and, second, for the most part, they tend to organize and operate as a separate community, especially the ultra-Orthodox.* I also left out Israeli Jews here because chapter 8 is devoted exclusively to Israel. However, more and more, their lifestyles, values, and self-understanding resemble their Jewish cousins in the United States, except they speak Hebrew (in addition to English) and they take off for Shabbat and Jewish holidays because most everything is closed there, except the beach.

The real question, then, regardless of whether we agree on the particulars of the description, is the following: "As presently constituted, does this community have the wherewithal to open the door and welcome those who have been 'other,' as well as those who do not currently feel connected, into our midst?" If so, we will thrive. If not, we

than religious. That same sensibility, however, was not fully passed down to their children growing up in North America who behave and believe just like their second- or third-generation contemporaries. Additionally, there are disadvantaged Jews (especially in Russia and the former Soviet Union) as well as members of tiny remnant communities in places like Egypt and Iran who do not, at all, fit this description of Diaspora Jews. But with the exception of Russia, their numbers are quite small.

*Interestingly, one time I was looking at the Art Scroll catalog and saw a translation of the *Mishna Berurah*, a rather obscure work of Jewish law written by Rabbi Yisrael Meir Kogan, better known as "the Chofetz Chaim." What immediately struck me was, why an English translation? Certainly, outside of the Orthodox community, very few if any Jews would have even heard of this work, let alone been interested in reading it! Could it be that the Hebrew skills of the potential readership are not good enough to tackle this work? And if so, what does that say about who they are becoming? We're not as separate or exclusive as we might have thought.

It reminded me of a childhood experience. I was walking with my grandfather on Eastern Parkway in Brooklyn, New York. Coming toward us from the opposite direction was a Hasid and his son. As we passed them, I heard the boy say in Yiddish, "*Gib a kook, tata . . . a Lassie hunt!*" ("Look Dad, a Lassie dog!") I turned around and saw a guy walking his collie. *Lassie* was then a popular television show. But how did he know about *Lassie*? Members of the Hasidic community didn't own television sets. The culture creeps in, no matter what.

will continue to decline. And in our decline, we run the risk of creating multiple parallel Jewish peoples and tons of dropouts as well—people who will be Jewish in name and DNA only, for whom their Jewish connection will be a curiosity at best but certainly not determinative of whom they choose to be in the world. As I have written previously, there is no certain future. Only the one we create. But of this I am certain: if we do not change now, the future will look a lot like the present, which means we will continue to decline, hunkering down in survival mode. Personally, I find that an unacceptable option. And I assume, since you are reading this book, you do as well.

This is the great challenge that lies before us—recreating the Jewish community that embraces and welcomes all who wish to join us as well as those who have, for one reason or another, become disenfranchised. And at the same time, we must keep those who have never left fully engaged and committed. I know this can feel daunting, even overwhelming. Many times in the course of my career I have heard comments from long-standing members like, "I don't know anyone around here anymore" or "I feel like a stranger in my own *shul*, the *shul* I helped build with my own hands!" I understand that. And I get how disconcerting it might be to suddenly feel like a stranger in one's own "home." The open door cannot be slammed in the face of those who have stayed the course.

It is a principle of group dynamics that people naturally form inner and outer circles when brought together in groups. We used to do this activity in our workshops designed for leaders of communities. We would give them a task like create a new game. The task itself was not the significant part of the exercise; rather, it was how they went about it that held the teaching moment. As soon as we handed out the task, we would observe their behavior. Some people formed a small circle and got right down to work; others watched and *kibitzed*; and still others drifted away, taking the opportunity to socialize, check their phones, and such. After a significant amount of time, we would freeze the action, asking people to observe where and why they were where they were in the room. The application to their various organizations was painfully apparent. Those on the inside felt "called" by the activity or responsible for its completion and, at the same time, were resentful of those who did not participate in the work, though they never asked or invited anyone to join them in doing so. The middle circle folks were interested to see how things worked out but did not feel it was theirs to create. Those on the outside felt displaced or bored, blaming the leaders of the exercise even though everyone had the same original choice. These participants were all leaders in their own organizations; nevertheless, when given an opportunity to not have to lead or participate, the majority was satisfied to allow others to take up the work on their behalf.

So this is what we know about groups, which we have to keep in mind if we wish to grow and thrive. When circles get bigger, current leadership will feel threatened as they become a smaller and smaller minority. And when minorities hold on to power—think of so many of the world's historical trouble spots like Syria, South Africa, Rwanda, colonial America—they will most often use force to oppress the majority. The real challenge is to always make certain that the door is open; that the circles are fluid and transparent; that moving from one place in the group to another is permitted, even encouraged and expected; that power and influence can be made accessible so as to be truly democratic and nonhierarchical; and that the legitimate concerns of all parties, even those on the periphery, are taken into serious consideration. People are truly happy when their gifts are valued and utilized, when they sense they are making a difference, and when they are appreciated for their efforts. Can our communities become a space where that is happening all the time for everyone? They will if we want to thrive.

I remember the first time I went to a food court in a mall. Having grown up in New York City, I really had never even seen a mall. There were, of course, many restaurant kiosks from which to choose, but only one had a very long line. So, of course, I wanted to check that one out. As I approached, I saw two people handing out little pieces of chicken on toothpicks. I did what everyone else did. I took my free sample, which was yummy, and got on line. The organized Jewish community has a great deal to learn from this model. Currently, we do the opposite. We have a "join first" mentality (which most often means donating or paying up front), and then we will take care of you.* This is a huge turnoff especially for young people used to getting everything for free from the internet, for interfaith families unused to the very idea of "joining" a church, or for any

---

*I cannot even begin to tell you the number of times people have come to me in tears or in anger because the first question they were asked when wishing to join a Jewish organization (especially synagogues) concerned how they were going to pay their dues.

person who grew up outside of North America where the government supports religious institutions. We have created many barriers without even realizing it. We have to change our model. Now.

The time is long past for us to lower the barriers, to get out of the safety and comfort of our buildings and campuses (which feel like fortresses to those on the outside) and go to where people are living their daily lives. In *Jewish Megatrends*, my friend Rabbi Sid Schwarz has come up with the suggestive concept of "micro-communities" to serve as a counterpoint to "transactional Judaism" (i.e., fee for service) that seems to be the popular easy way out to "do" Jewish without having to take seriously "being" Jewish.[2] Dues mean they "owe us" something. Nobody owes the Jewish community anything anymore. That model died with the *shtetls* in Europe. We have to shed that mentality, or we will die angry and sad. Like that food court kiosk, we have to trust that what we have is of great enough importance, meaning, and quality that we can afford to give it away. The support will come afterward. Or, as I have heard it said, when the "why" is strong, the "how" will reveal itself. Like it or not, today we have to have a "why," or we will become irrelevant. "Do it for your *bubbe* and *zayde*!" or "Do it because of all those Jews who perished in the Holocaust!" might have worked once upon a time. Yes, guilt can be a motivator. News flash! It does not work anymore. Jews know why they go to yoga, or work out, or hang out at Happy Hour after work on Friday. Ask them. They will tell you. Today they need to know why they should be Jewish as well, or even care about it. And, if after four thousand years we cannot supply a compelling answer, then shame on us!*

Over the years of my active rabbinate, I heard a lot of complaints and whining about Chabad, especially from pulpit rabbis. Instead of complaining, they should have been taking notes. I don't know about being the *Mashiach*, but the Rebbe was a genius. He understood the contemporary world and positioned his organization to become incredibly effective and successful. I know. My early education was at his Lubavitch School, Talmud Torah of Eastern Parkway, and the then young, soon to be great

---

*I propose the following as a starting point: Judaism, one of the world's oldest religions, is the greatest system I know for individual and planetary transformation, enriching our lives with sacred meaning and purpose, providing for a sense of individual wholeness and inner peace, and strengthening us as a community while creating a world of justice and love for all people everywhere. That's just my opinion. I welcome others.

Rabbi Marlowe was my teacher. So here is what Chabad gets that the rest of the Jewish world needs to learn:

1. Relationship, relationship, relationship. Relationship is the foundation for *all* accomplishment. Build the relationship first, and the rest will follow.
2. One *mitzvah* at a time. Celebrate every success, no matter how small.
3. Give it away (and ask for support later). No dues. No membership.
4. Go to where the people are—streets, airports, offices, hospitals.
5. Stay on mission, always (even if no one is paying attention).
6. Hand-picked, recruited, supported, and developed leadership—the "best of the best."
7. Local leaders (the rabbi and *rebbetzin*) need to both be completely committed to the cause and always, unashamedly, themselves.
8. True acceptance and love of each and every Jew.
9. Local leaders are responsible (franchise model).
10. Most Jews are not religious but are happy that their rabbi is. Accept it. Get over it.

I am not here suggesting that the Chabad organization can be duplicated, or even serve as a model for the entire Jewish world. After all, this is a highly centralized, even autocratic leadership built around the charisma and unquestioned power of one person, who continues to be the focus of their work even long after his death. Local Chabad houses have no boards of directors and so all decisions rest with the local rabbi leader. Further, Chabad does "in-reach" only because the first thing they ask you is, "Are you Jewish?" If your answer is "no" they tend to leave you alone (unless they have done some prior research on you). Chabad's mission is to deepen the Jewish experience by doing certain powerful, sensory, entry-level *mitzvot*—namely, putting on *t'fellin* (phylacteries) for men, and lighting Shabbat candles for women. Of course, they have a number of other programs, like the Friendship Circle, with deep impact. However, they are not interested in conversion, nor do they actively recruit people to become Lubavitchers. In other words, other than having large families, they are not interested in growing the Jewish people. Further, their premodern way of life will not appeal to large swaths of contemporary Jews. Vicarious Judaism (i.e., "I am not religious but if I was I would be like them"), no matter how good it feels personally, is hardly likely to create a thriving community. A cynic might say their number one interest is building "friends of Chabad," friends with large bank accounts. Nevertheless, they are highly successful and for good reason. We can all learn from what they have accomplished.

If we want to build the community of the future, we need, first and foremost, to reach out to everyone with true curiosity. Having an "open" sign is not nearly enough—nor is the attitude, too often prevalent among the insiders of our communities, "They know where we are . . . if they want to be part of us, they know where to find us." As we have learned from the field of appreciative inquiry, connecting with others begins with positive, probing questions, not problems, demands, expectations, or even requests.* We need to connect with people's strengths and gifts and to the issues that move them, that mean something to them, and that they care about. We need to want to hear about their images of the future, the ones that give them a sense of purpose and fulfillment. We want to let them know that being Jewish is not only about supporting one another— "grooving together," to use a 1960s term—but it means building something for our world. That is what Judaism has always been about. We may call them *mitzvot* (commandments), but really they are opportunities to make a difference within us and between us, in our lives and in the life of the world itself.

Thousands of years ago, a solo couple, Avram and Sarai (as they were then named)—the first Jewish "converts"—listened to their inner voice and the voice of God and set out on a journey that would change them forever while transforming the world. According to the rabbis, Avram experienced ten trials, the most famous of which was the binding of his son Isaac for sacrifice. These stories are recorded in the Torah not as his-

---

*One group that is using this approach with great effect is Makom on Long Island, New York, which calls itself an "intentional community." We need to encourage and support more such efforts. Hadar, an online learning platform, has launched Project Zug, which promotes *havruta*-style (usually meaning two people paired together) study connecting Jews across the world. OneTable encourages Shabbat dinner experiences combining ancient ritual with current personal beliefs, experiences, and passions. Detroit's Jews for Justice unites Jewish activisits. These are just some of the efforts afoot that are not just a new technology; rather, they are helping us create a new way of seeing/understanding community while transforming traditional formats to enhance and sustain Jewish life experience.

torical events; rather, they are meant as life lessons. Each of us is tested and challenged in life. It is not about getting an "A" each time. Instead, it is about learning and growing so that we can become the best version of ourselves. Along the way, Avram's name is changed to Abraham and Sarai's is changed to Sarah. The letter "h" in English is the letter "hey" in Hebrew. "Hey" is an abbreviation for God's name. Both of them had God added to their names, just as it had in their lives. When we align our individual purpose in life with God's true purpose for us, however we understand that, we are transformed and we bring positive transformation into the world.

After millennia of surviving, miraculously overcoming the odds of history that would have assigned us to the ash heap of dead religions and extinct peoples, we are once again called upon to bring such transformation into the world, fulfilling our true purpose. We are called upon to create communities that support us and our loved ones spiritually, emotionally, intellectually, and physically while giving us a true voice. My son, Ezra, who is the artistic director for Lab/Shul, an alternative Jewish experience in New York, calls it "dangerous Judaism," a Judaism that shakes us, challenges us even while it supports us in our striving and experimentation. It's a Judaism that helps us escape from the boredom, repetition, "doing things the way they have always been done," and rote ritual that is unfortunately the common fare in our Jewish institutions today. It's a Judaism that dials down the over-intellectualization and left-brain thinking that has dominated our tradition for centuries, while dialing up matters of the heart and spirit (like meditation and prayer) and, yes, the body as well. It's a Judaism that does away with the distortion of the Golden Rule (i.e., the one who has the gold, rules) that continues to dominate the important decision making across the Jewish world, limiting access to new and fresh ideas. My teacher of blessed memory, Rabbi Eugene Borowitz, coined the term "covenantal community" to describe a purpose-centered community linked by something greater than mere tribal connection.[3] This is the essence of what it means for us to thrive.*

---

*There are many postmodern Jews who describe their "faith" as "Tribal Judaism" or what we may have once called "peoplehood." Such an approach may connect us one to the other. It may strengthen our commitment to group identity. And there always has to be a place at the table for those who self-identify in this way. But Tribal Judaism can never bring us true purpose for our existence. For that, we need Judaism itself, but not just the same old, same old.

Though the term "*tikkun olam*" has its origins in the mystical works of the *Kabbalah* with meaning that has cosmic implications, today it has come to refer to all those actions we take to make the world a better place for all of us. The contemporary Jewish educator Joel Grishaver referred to us as "fixers," Jewish repairmen and women involved in issues of social justice and social action.[4] Whether your passion is in ending poverty, hunger, or homelessness; providing access to quality health care and education; eliminating inequality; sustainable cities, responsible consumption, renewable energy, clean water, and sanitation; climate action; gender safety; gun control; good jobs and healthy, fairly distributed economic growth; inclusive societies; or peace and justice, you are aligning yourself with the highest aims of our tradition. While perfection is out of the reach of us imperfect human beings, we are required to bring goodness into the world, for ourselves, for all the ones we love, and for all of humanity. Loving our neighbor (and in the global world in which we live we are all neighbors) means wanting for them the same that we want for ourselves. Two thousand years ago Rabbi Hillel expounded that this principle is the essence of the Torah, and the rest is commentary. Let's follow his counsel and learn it. Let's live it.*

In an effort to save and serve ourselves, we created institutions, which is understandable. We proudly call it community, but in reality, as currently constituted, we are separate silo organizations that too often see and act toward each other as competitors. True, I have seen us come together in times of crisis or when tragedy strikes. In those moments, we lay aside our differences and work for the common good. Those are the times we turn to one another and ask, "Why can't it be like this all the time?" It is a truism that when we look at the world and see scarcity—limited resources, human and material—we go to our default position of survival. After all, we humans are animals, the latest and least evolved on the planet. Fight or flight is built into our very DNA as well as our brain chemistry. On the other hand, if we look at the world as a place of abundance—there is enough for everybody—then we can cooperate and all of us thrive.

The present-day Jewish establishment is resigned to scarcity—fewer people, fewer funds, fewer resources—and so we must compete or die.

---

*Hillel actually phrased his interpretation of Love your Neighbor in the negative. He said, "What is hateful to you, do not do to others." In other words, refrain from doing harm. Not a bad idea!

And with such a mentality, ironically, we will continue to witness the demise of those very institutions we created to enhance Jewish life and continuity. For after all, that is what resignation does to us. It defeats us. And it sends a negative message to all those who are watching from the sidelines. Whether or not they realize it, the Jewish establishment is playing the dangerous game of last institution standing. And the more day schools that close their doors, synagogues that have to merge, Jewish hospitals that have to sell to their originally Christian counterparts, and national organizations that downsize staff, programs, and services, we see the "proof" of that scarcity mentality. This is a self-fulfilling prophecy if ever there was one.

But what if we reimagined ourselves as a real community in which the legitimate needs of all its members had to be considered?[5] What if we now understood that our real task is to serve (and some would say, save) the world? What if we approached this challenge with the sure belief that there are enough resources and people out there for that to happen? Then, the very nature and structure of the Jewish community would have to evolve. Instead of spending all of our energy and resources propping up the institutions that already exist, sadly watching and clucking our tongues as pieces die and fade away and, at the same time, funding new ones with exciting programs that are now competing with the already established organizations that look upon them with hostility and suspicion, we would ask ourselves, "What would a thriving Jewish community look like, and what structures (if any) do we need to realize that goal?" If some of them already exist, then all we need to do is align them with a "thrival" agenda. We might also need to create new ones that are light and flexible, for the world is changing rapidly. Did you know that the largest "hotel" chain in the world today does not own one room—Airbnb; and the largest "cab" company does not own a single car—Uber? We have to be similarly creative. And we will undoubtedly realize that we have lots of redundancy in the institutions we already have, and so they will need to unite their efforts for the sake of a shared mission, for the sake of our people, for the sake of the world. Right now, the proverbial tail (our already existing institutions) is wagging the dog (the people and the community). That has to be reversed if we are to thrive.

In 2017, I attended a performance of the Miami Ballet Company. The very next day I received an e-mail from the theater thanking me for attending together with a short survey requesting my feedback. My immediate thought was "Imagine getting one of these from my synagogue after the High Holy Days!" It might read something like this, *Dear Rabbi Bookman, thank you for joining with us in creating a sacred community during these last High Holy Days. Please take a moment to respond to the enclosed survey. We need to hear from our community so that we can serve you all better. And once again, may your year be filled with goodness and blessing!* That would be a real "Wow!" But it is not just the synagogues. I make a small donation to a secular organization or that of another faith tradition and quickly receive a thank-you, often with a handwritten note. I make a much larger donation to a Jewish cause, and if I hear back at all, it is usually accompanied by yet another solicitation urging me to give even more next time.

In order to thrive, we must begin with the admission that what we are currently doing is *not* working. Why? If it was a product we were selling (remember big cars from Detroit automakers) that was now obsolete, that no one wanted anymore, we would probably have to shut down the company, taking the product off the market, no matter how good or popular it once was. For those of us who love Judaism that is simply not an option we wish to entertain. But if we are being honest with ourselves, we have to admit that our "customers" are not satisfied, and unless we do real market research to find out why, to really listen (not argue) to what they have to say, and then make the necessary adjustments, letting go of some, if not all of our "sacred cows," we will continue to lose "market share." We insiders still believe in our product. It is time tested, and we know it works. Does it need repackaging? A new and improved version? Or, as has been argued since modernity began, is religion an antiquated modality to respond to life's big questions? Does it need to be replaced by science and psychology? Though I love and learn from both of them, I hope that is not the case. What I do know is this: we need to ask the tough questions, and we need to hear from those who currently appear to be disinterested, including our own children.

In a real community, we work together for the legitimate needs of *all* members, not just the insiders, the *machers* (big shots or power brokers), and the professional staffers. The current Jewish community in most of the world operates as a group of silos with its number one goal of keeping each silo intact. The former offers us the opportunity to thrive; the latter is destined to die, a slow death that we are currently witnessing as the contents of each silo (people, resources) continue to shrink. I do not know exactly what the Open Door community will look like. And if I did, it would only represent me, not us. But what I do know is that we have the talent, intelligence, and capacity to reorganize as one worldwide community working together for the good of all. I also know that such a massive effort is necessary, even essential, if we are going to thrive. While there will inevitably be some dropouts—there always are when change is undertaken—such a community will reinvigorate those who have remained steadfast and loyal. At the same time, it will draw new energy, creativity, purpose, and people to our ancient and still sacred task.

Beyond Survival

An Afterword

𝓘 fully suspect that this book will be met with lots of skepticism. Many naysayers will announce that it has never been done this way before, so why should we start now? After all, against all the odds of history, we are still here, going strong. Jews and Judaism are powerful contributors to practically every society in which we live. We are successful, well educated, and well connected. All true. Others will say Rabbi Bookman is naive and unrealistic. I have been hearing those kinds of comments my entire life. I'm not worried, though. I have been called a lot worse. And, of course, there will be others who disagree both with my assessment of the current status of the worldwide Jewish community, as well as my suggested alternative solutions. I fully welcome these conversations. Judaism is a dialectic tradition; it is how we do Judaism! My only hope is that these will be disagreements *b'shem shamayim* (literally "for the sake of heaven"), meaning for the benefit of all people everywhere and not simply to satisfy someone's personal agenda.*

Of course, writing a book like this is preceded by many conversations. Some of the ideas here were tested in my Torah study community at Temple Beth Am in Miami. The open and honest dialogue we shared for more than twenty years never failed to challenge me and make me think and rethink my stance on any number of issues. Hopefully, it made me a better teacher and a better person. You will have to ask them.

---

*Pirke Avot 5:20 states, "Every argument that is for the sake of heaven will be sustained; on the other hand, if it is an ego-driven argument, it will not be sustained."

As I shared chapters of the rough draft of this manuscript, seeking their feedback as well as wisdom, some friends have questioned, "Okay, I am convinced—we need to do this. But how can we get this done? How can we get the Jewish community to thrive? You say your teaching is never theoretical, right? So tell us practically, how do we do this?" To tell you the truth, I had no intention of responding to the "How?" question. My book, as the subtitle indicates, is intended to be a new vision for the worldwide Jewish community. Vision statements are usually the work of a single individual, a leader, the CEO of an organization, meant to answer the question, "Where are we going?" In the vetting and sharing of the vision, inevitably these statements need to address "*Why* do we need to go there?" or "*What* are the underlying values or principles in this choice of direction?" I hope I did an adequate job in explaining just what we need to do and why we need to do it, and especially why we need to do so now. How to get there is sometimes called a "Strategic Plan," most often the work of a group of decision makers and leaders. A strategic plan is meant to take us, step by step, toward the realization of the vision. For example, if I declared, "We are going to New York!" the family would get together and decide how we would travel, when we would leave, where we would stay, and what we might do once we got there. That's a plan!

Nevertheless, my friends' question—How are we going to get there?—began to gnaw at me.

One more thing. In this book, I have written about how the Jewish people and Judaism can thrive. That should not come as a shock to anyone. After all, I am a Jew and a rabbi who has spent more than half my life working on behalf of my people. Besides, Judaism is what I know, my grounding; it is the spiritual and intellectual place from which I approach all of life—hopefully, my area of expertise. To borrow the words of Howard Bogot, I see the world through Jewish eyes.[1]

But I also know this: we live in an interconnected world. Though we value our freedoms and independence, none of us is an isolated individual; rather, we are all a part of a greater, integrated whole. We are, in fact, truly one. What I do in my small corner of the globe impacts and is felt everywhere. To work for a thriving community at the expense or exclusion of another group of people is a lose-lose. It alienates the other while truly diminishing us at the same time. Religions (and nations) have been doing so for far too long, and it has given religion a well-earned black eye while weakening trust and workability. Anytime my success comes at the expense of another, it is bound to be temporary, illusory, and short lived. We all need to "*grok*" or understand and internalize that life lesson. Only that which speaks to the needs of all concerned parties is worthy of our time and effort.

What follows, then, is my initial response to the "How?" question. And it is my hope that it will serve as a call to action, a first step on the way to fulfillment and truly thriving as a worldwide community of faith and hope.

In the creation story of our people, we learn that everything takes on reality with a word. God may have thought of creation for billions of years. God may have imagined what creation would look like and even might have had blueprints drawn. God may even have discussed the concept with the ministering angels.* However, until the word is pronounced—let there be "X"—nothing exists. This is, of course, a life lesson, not an alternative scientific accounting, not a replacement to the Big Bang, not some half-baked "creationism." We all, each and every one of us, generate thousands of ideas in the course of our lifetime, but very few of them become actualized. In fact, the Torah teaches us, the only ideas that have even a chance of coming into creation are the ones we are willing to take the risk to name. In this book, I have attempted to name a better future for my people and, by extension, for all people everywhere. Originally, I named it "thrival" to indicate that it is something that does not yet exist, but my publisher thought it would be too confusing, so we named this book, *Beyond Survival.* Decline as a community is not inevitable. It only comes about when leadership is resigned to a present that is failing. In the theater in Telluride, Colorado, named for the artist and illustrator Chuck Jones, there is a quote attributed to him that says, "For those who are willing to think, there is no inevitable." Hopefully, this book has got you thinking.

All great movements begin with a word, and then a conversation. In fact, I would say, nothing great has ever happened in this world without being preceded by multiple conversations. For those of us who believe in "thrival," the next step is to begin a conversation, one on one, or in thrival

---

*If you like this kind of speculation, you may be ready to be a Kabbalist. This kind of speculative philosophy, getting into the mind of God, is the very stuff of Jewish mysticism, especially the strand known as Four Worlds.

groups. This can be done in person, the old-fashioned way, or through social media. We want everyone to join in on this conversation, bringing together people with religious backgrounds and strong Jewish identity as well as those who never step inside a Jewish organization. We want market people and financial wizards; philosophers, artists, teachers, and learners; outsiders and outliers; scholars and beginners; donors, entrepreneurs, and venture capitalists; young and old; and everyone in between. Everyone has something to add. My suggested agenda is a single question: How can we thrive? My one operating principle (one that I learned from Peter Block) is that everyone we need is already in the "room." In other words, given all the various connections each of us has, we have everyone we need to figure this out. And my one caveat is that anything and everything can be discussed. There can be no limitations to these conversations; no topic or question or opinion is off limits. And hard questions have to be asked: Why are we shrinking? Why is participation in the Jewish community often such a negative turnoff? Why do so many Jews go elsewhere for their spiritual needs? Why, if Judaism is so great, do we have trouble passing it down to our children? Be that said, my guess is that each thrival group will more than likely come up with different answers to our questions and even create some new questions that we have not yet thought of. That's not a problem. After all, right now, this opportunity to thrive exists only in our imagined future. Besides, different micro-communities might have different needs. After a time, when thrival groups start to get together to examine the larger challenges, they will inevitably consolidate their efforts and decisions. I have faith that, together, we can figure this out. We can get to the "yes" of thrival when that is our true collective goal.* And, in point of fact, just having the conversations is already creating the thriving community, already bringing it into existence.

I wrote earlier in this book that I once interviewed for a position, and when I looked around the room, I noticed that every person at the table had a long history of volunteer commitment for the organization.

---

*The premise of the marvelous book *Getting to Yes*, by Roger Fisher and William Ury, is that when parties agree on the final outcome, the negotiation on how to get there is a very different process and experience (Roger Fisher and William Ury, *Getting to Yes: Negotiating Agreement without Giving In*, rev. ed. [New York: Penguin, 2001]). If we all agree that we want a thriving community, the road might be long, but it will be quite smooth. Right now, the worldwide Jewish community is preparing for decline, even demise, as if that is inevitable. My audacious retort is, "Who said so?!"

Yet the conversation we were having was about the "young people" who were not there. When I pointed out this paradox, I was met with a rather paternalistic attitude of, "Rabbi, we know best." Everyone at the interview certainly deserved to be there. They earned their seat at the table, so to speak. Nevertheless, if we want their involvement and commitment, we also need to hear from those who are not currently at the table; for after all, their numbers keep growing, and today they represent the majority of Jews—the ones who say they are "just Jewish" on every survey. In other words, thrival groups need to include everyone who chooses to be there while reaching out to those who never thought they would. We need to speak to baby boomers who drop out once their children become *Bar* or *Bat Mitzvah* or leave home. We need to find out why those children, even those who had strong Jewish upbringings, do not choose to return, are opting out, are seeking alternative communities, or are just plain not interested anymore. Perhaps they, too, believe their voices and ideas do not matter because "we know best."

In this book, I have suggested the broad outlines of what a thriving Jewish community might look like. Each chapter proposed a different piece of a thrival vision. It began with the obstacles that currently stand in our way. There are always obstacles to change; this should not surprise us. They can stop us in our tracks, convince us to give up, and fake us into believing we are defeated even before we begin. However, I have learned from experience that there is no obstacle that cannot be surmounted, especially when we work together for a common purpose. We can go over them, around them, under them, or simply blow them up. As Winston Churchill once said, "A pessimist sees the difficulty in every opportunity; an optimist sees the opportunity in every difficulty."[2] Each of our current obstacles to thrival represent the past. The past is never forgotten, but we have learned that we can no longer afford to simply repeat it. History cannot be changed. What is done, is done. We appreciate the past and all that it has done to define us, but just like a leader completing his/her term of service, he/she has to step down so that new leadership can emerge. When organizations practice STP (same ten people), they choke off the opportunity for new people to step up, all the while complaining that "no one wants to do anything around here." When a community, an organization, a business, or even an individual continues to do the same thing ad infinitum, they die a slow death, for the one truth of all life is that it is changing all the time. Perhaps ironically, change is the only constant in the universe. To resist change (which can often feel sad or scary) is to court certain death.

What are the changes we need to incorporate? Well, it begins with an admission that what we are currently doing, no matter how much we love it, no matter how meaningful it might be for us individually, no matter how much it honors our loved ones and the gifts of the past, is simply not working. You know the joke, "How many Jews does it take to change a light bulb? Change? My grandparents donated that light bulb!" I have suggested that we need to grow our numbers and that the opportunity to do so is at our very fingertips. Growth of the Jewish people can occur by welcoming the emerging Jewish communities around the globe, both those who are returning as well as those who miraculously never really left. We can grow through active conversion, reaching out to the millions of searchers around the globe looking for a spiritual home. We can grow by making room in the tent for the now millions or more people who practice another faith or no faith at all but who are part of our extended family through marriage or close friendship, instead of making them feel like pariahs who are destroying Judaism. I remember when we began to turn around a membership decline at my synagogue with lots of new members, one of the regulars said, "I don't know anyone anymore. I feel like a stranger in my own synagogue." I know he was speaking a painful emotional truth. Those of us who have been on the inside need to make room in our organizations and our hearts for newcomers to join us. Yes, at first, it will feel different, but in time, it will no longer feel strange. It will become the new normal.

But it is not merely a numbers game. We need to remember that Judaism is a system for personal and planetary transformation leading to a life of meaning, purpose, and holiness. We need to reinvigorate our common purpose of making the world a better place for all people everywhere, to be a light in a world that is too often dark—the eternal "why" of the Jewish people. Such dedication, I am convinced, will help ignite the spark of Jewish identity and activism that is now dimming in the millennial generation. Our children and grandchildren no longer automatically check off the Jewish option as did previous generations who actually had no option to do otherwise. Those of us who are committed to Jewish continuity need to understand this. We have to really get it. Unless our children and grandchildren have a meaningful answer to why be Jewish, they may not officially drop out, but they will not actively drop in. Judaism will become a DNA piece of their total identity, a curiosity at best, but not something that will motivate their time, resources, or personal commitment.

The structures that have sustained the Jewish community—synagogues, Jewish Federations, Jewish Community Centers, so-called secular organizations, among others—have to become more flexible and interconnected and much more local. We have way too many silos out there. And we may not have enough of the "right" structures. As I said previously, when the "why" is clear, the "how" will follow. But one thing is clear. Our current faux community is unsustainable, and if we continue to play the dangerous game of "last one standing," we will soon be asking someone to turn out the lights as we "tsk tsk/oy vey" our way into oblivion.

And finally, Israel has the opportunity to live up to its potential as the true home of *all* the Jewish people, both those who live there as well as those of us who visit (or as it has been said, who are making *alliyah* in stages). The world is watching our tiny nation. Its decisions are important. As it has done in the realms of technology, medicine, and business, Israel must fully own its transition from the fledgling and fragile precarious state it once was to the powerful role model it has gratefully become. The Diaspora and Israel are inextricably tied one to the other. We will rise or fall together. We can never afford to lose interest in and connection with one another.

On a visit to Israel in fall 2016, I participated in a *Kabbalat Shabbat* at the old railway station in Jerusalem together with a wide and varied group of *daveners* and onlookers. There were people, young and old, wearing traditional garb as well as bikers and roller skaters. The inspiring group of musicians and singers led us in a new *Oseh Shalom*. But not only was the melody different (imagine that), but there was also a new phrase added to the words. In addition to wishing peace to us, and all of Israel, we were asking God to bring peace to *kol yoshvei tayvel*—to all the inhabitants of the earth. And then it dawned on me. Of course! How can we Jews have peace (i.e., wholeness) unless and until everyone else does as well? We are all of us interconnected. I believe the same is true with thriving. *Beyond Survival* is not just about the Jews doing better. It is about all of us living in a better world. All of us growing. All of us reaching our full potential and supporting one another in the process. The late Reverend Martin Luther King Jr. said it best:

All I'm saying is simply this: that all mankind is tied together; all life is interrelated, and we are all caught in an inescapable network of mutuality, tied in a single garment of destiny. Whatever affects one directly, affects all indirectly. For some strange reason I can never be what I ought to be until you are what you ought to be. And you can never be what you ought to be unless I am what I ought to be—this is the interrelated structure of reality.[3]

A world of thrival!

That's it. I both welcome and look forward to your comments on how we can thrive. Connect with me at tuvyah@eitzah.org or on Facebook. I personally respond to each and every communication. Together is the only way forward. Together let us thrive.

P.S. Writing a book, any book, is a multiyear process. This one is no exception. What that has afforded me is the opportunity to engage others in a thrival conversation, a kind of head start to what I suggest in this afterword. Out of those conversations I formulated a number of questions that help both individuals as well as organizations determine if they have created a climate or culture of thrival. I include them here for you personally or for any organization to which you are committed. Feel free to share them with all the ones you love.

THRIVAL CHECKLIST (FOR INDIVIDUALS)

What are my gifts?
Are my gifts being fully utilized?
What am I passionate about?
What is my personal mission?
Am I making a difference in the world?
Do I feel appreciated for what I do? At work? At "home"?
Do I see the world as a place of scarcity (not enough to go around) or plenty (enough for everyone)?
Do I approach life with an attitude of gratitude?
Do I feel awe when I think of the world in which we live?
Do I give and receive love each day?

How do I take care of myself (physically, emotionally, intellectually, and spiritually)?

Am I generous with my time? With my financial resources?

Can I accept the things I cannot change?

Is there anyone I (still) need to forgive (including myself)?

How do I bounce back from setbacks and loss?

THRIVAL CHECKLIST
(FOR COMMUNITIES AND ORGANIZATIONS)

What is our mission? Are we living into it (i.e., are all community decisions made with the mission in mind)?

Where is our vision taking us over the next five years?

How are visitors/newcomers welcomed?

Do we know and fully utilize everyone's (professionals, volunteers) gifts?

How do we demonstrate appreciation for each person's contributions?

Does our website reflect who we are? Who we want to be?

How do we cultivate new leadership? Or do we practice STP (same ten people), complaining that "no one wants to take responsibility around here"?

Are we growing or shrinking? What are the contributing factors?

Are we financially stable? Responsible?

Are decisions made with transparency?

How do people make their voices heard? Are we listening to everyone's concerns?

Do our physical facilities adequately reflect our day-to-day needs?

Are we fully resilient in the way we deal with setbacks and loss?

If you did not already have a connection, would you create one with this organization/community? Why or why not?

Acknowledgments

$\mathcal{T}$his book would not have been written without the encouragement of Noreen Gordon Sablotsky. When I was foundering, she saw the passion I had for this topic and told me to just start writing. Having successfully published four books, and knowing the amount of work it takes to "birth one," I figured I was done. Thankfully, I listened to her, and the words poured out of me; she read each and every chapter with her careful suggestions. And here are the results. If you are moved by this book, thank her.

Many people read chapters and offered their critiques—my sons Ariel, Jonah, Micah, and Ezra each came with the perspective of young, committed Jews who are both shaping and finding their ways into the Jewish community of today, while creating it anew for the future. Additionally, Ariel served as my format editor. His careful reading and watchful eye challenged me, helping me avoid some embarrassing mistakes while getting the manuscript ready for submission. Thanks to him, editing was not the torture it has been for me in the past.

Good friends Larry Suchman, Steve Raymund, and Dick Golden were continuous cheerleaders as well as critical readers. Their friendship and support, especially in a project like this, meant the world to me. My former agent, Julie Merberg, was instrumental in both her guidance and knowledge of the publishing world. Always helpful, always enthusiastic, Julie has been "in my corner" from day one of my book writing career. I cannot thank her enough.

I also want to thank my amazing group of peer reviewers who gave their time, critical reading, and insight to the initial stage of this project: Professor Tudor Parfitt, whose groundbreaking work in identifying the emerging global Jewish communities is literally changing the face of Judaism; Rabbi Sid Schwarz, the "innovator-in-chief" who continues to push the envelope of what is possible for the Jewish people and has been a friend and mentor; Dr. Ellen Silverman, a sensitive artist, gifted therapist, and author of truly inclusive Jewish books; Rabbi Rachel Greengrass, already one of modern Judaism's most passionate and compassionate rabbis; and Rabbi Dan Horwitz, who, through his inclusion, commitment, and dedication, expands the paradigm of what we believe is possible for Judaism and our people. I am truly fortunate to have these hearts, minds, and souls in my corner.

Rolf Janke, Courtney Packard, Janice Braunstein, and the entire team at Rowman & Littlefield believed in this project from its inception. I am honored to have such a "giant" of publishing behind my work.

Many of the ideas fully expressed in this work had their genesis in the Beth Am Torah study group that I was blessed to teach every Shabbat over a period of twenty years. The hundreds of serious Jews I encountered each week, who both listened to and challenged me made me a better teacher and, hopefully, a better human being. I thank them from the depth of my heart. They know who they are.

And finally, I want to thank the public relations firm My City Social for helping me raise my voice. From the time I met Michael Gonzalez, I knew I wanted to work with them to return to the public arena, after an absence of more than three years. I thank Paula Palacios, my media guru, and their team for all that they have done.

Notes

BEYOND SURVIVAL: A NEW JEWISH VISION

1. Jonathan Safran Foer, *Here I Am* (New York: Farrar, Straus & Giroux, 2016).
2. Ari Goldman, "Dalai Lama Meets Jews from Four Major Branches," *New York Times*, September 26, 1989, B4, https://www.nytimes.com/1989/09/26/nyregion/dalai-lama-meets-jews-from-4-major-branches.html.
3. Spencer Johnson, *Who Moved My Cheese? An Amazing Way to Deal with Change in Your Work and in Your Life* (New York: Putnam, 1998).
4. Dean Burnett, *Idiot Brain: What Your Head Is Really Up To* (New York: Norton, 2016), 27.

CHAPTER 1: THE BIG THREE PLUS ONE

1. Katrin Bennhold, "One Legacy of Merkel? Angry East German Men Fueling the Far Right," *New York Times*, November 5, 2018.
2. Max Weber, *The Protestant Ethic and the Spirit of Capitalism*, trans. Talcott Parsons (New York: Scribner, 1958).
3. William Faulkner, *Requiem for a Nun* (New York: Vintage, 2011), 69.
4. Lesli Koppelman Ross, "The Importance of Remembering," My Jewish Learning, https://www.myjewishlearning.com/article/the-importance-of-remembering.
5. *Talk of the Nation*, hosted by Neal Conan, NPR, December 8, 2008; Avraham Burg, *The Holocaust Is Over: We Must Rise from Its Ashes* (New York: Palgrave Macmillan, 2008).
6. Mitch Landrieu, "On the Removal of Four Confederate Monuments in New Orleans" (speech, Gallier Hall, New Orleans, LA, May 19, 2017).

7. Adina Allen, "'Is, Was, Will Be,'" *Sh'ma Now: A Journal of Jewish Sensibilities*, February 12, 2017, https://forward.com/shma-now/chidush/362685/39-is-was-will-be39.

8. Do you know that the top eighteen Jewish not-for-profit executives made more than a half million dollars each in 2016? And the next fifteen are not that far behind. Steven Davidson, "How Much Do Top Jewish Non-Profit Leaders Make?," *Forward*, December 11, 2017, https://forward.com/news/388240/how-much-do-top-jewish-non-profit-leaders-make.

9. Ross Douthat, "The Jewish Crossroads," *New York Times*, August 4, 2018, https://www.nytimes.com/2018/08/04/opinion/sunday/steven-m-cohen-jewish-crossroads.html.

CHAPTER 2: AN UGLY TRUTH

1. Ruth Eglash, "A 70-Year-Old Mystery: Yemini Jews Say Young Relatives Were Stolen in Israel," *Washington Post*, August 8, 2016, https://www.washingtonpost.com/world/middle_east/a-70-year-old-mystery-yemeni-jews-say-young-relatives-were-stolen-in-israel/2016/08/05/385c8d4f-0831-48a9-aaba-a3c9ff3c275c_story.html?utm_term=.d93300ce41f5.

2. Hadas Fuchs and Gilad Brand, "Education and Employment Trends among Ethiopian Israelis," Taub Center for Social Policy Studies in Israel, June 2015, http://taubcenter.org.il/wp-content/files_mf/ethiopianeducationandemployment2015english.pdf.

3. Ben Sales, "New President Seeks to Cure 'Epidemic' of Racism," *Times of Israel*, October 24, 2015, https://www.timesofisrael.com/new-president-seeks-to-cure-disease-of-racism.

4. Robert Kurzban, John Tooby, and Leda Cosmides, "Can Race Be Erased? Coalitional Computation and Social Categorization," *Proceedings of the National Academy of Sciences* 98, no. 26 (December 18, 2001): 15387–92, https://doi.org/10.1073/pnas.251541498.

5. Dante A. Puzzo, "Racism and the Western Tradition," *Journal of the History of Ideas* 25, no. 4 (October–December 1964), 579–86.

6. Hannah Arendt, *The Origins of Totalitarianism* (New York: Harcourt, Brace, 1951).

7. Joel Kovel, *White Racism: A Psychohistory* (New York: Pantheon, 1970).

8. Mitch Landrieu, "On the Removal of Four Confederate Monuments in New Orleans" (speech, Gallier Hall, New Orleans, LA, May 19, 2017).

9. Gurdeep Parhar, "Fixing Racism" (lecture, TEDxStanleyPark, Vancouver, BC, May 28, 2016), https://www.tedxstanleypark.com/speakers/2016-2.

CHAPTER 3: WHO IS A JEW?

1. Antonio Regalado, "2017 Was the Year Consumer DNA Testing Blew Up," *MIT Technology Review*, February 12, 2018, https://www.technologyreview.com/s/610233/2017-was-the-year-consumer-dna-testing-blew-up.
2. Amanda Borschel-Dan, "Will New Conversion Bill Help 400,000 Israelis of 'No Religion'? Not Likely," *Times of Israel*, April 24, 2018, https://www.timesofisrael.com/will-new-conversion-bill-help-400000-israelis-of-no-religion-not-likely.

CHAPTER 4: DO THE MATH!

1. "Iran: We Will Help 'Cut Out the Cancer of Israel,'" *Telegraph*, February 3, 2012, https://www.telegraph.co.uk/news/worldnews/middleeast/iran/9059179/Iran-We-will-help-cut-out-the-cancer-of-Israel.html.
2. Greg Tepper, "Israel a 'Cancerous Tumor' and Middle East's Biggest Problem, Iranian Supreme Leader Says," *Times of Israel*, August 19, 2012, http://www.timesofisrael.com/khamenei-israeli-a-malignant-zionist-tumor.
3. Stephen Covey, *The 7 Habits of Highly Effective People* (New York: Simon & Schuster, 1989).
4. *Yorah Deah* 268:2, *Sephoria*.

CHAPTER 5: A FUNNY THING HAPPENED TO ME ON MY WAY TO MIAMI

1. Suzanne Selengut, "The Converso Comeback," *Tablet Magazine*, October 17, 2017, https://www.tabletmag.com/jewish-life-and-religion/246057/the-converso-comeback.
2. Nathan P. Devir, *New Children of Israel: Emerging Jewish Communities in an Era of Globalization* (Salt Lake City: University of Utah Press, 2017).
3. Genie Milgrom, *My 15 Grandmothers* (Lexington, KY: G. Milgrom, 2012).

CHAPTER 6: LOVE VERSUS LOYALTY

1. "Orthodox Group Forms Unit to Combat Intermarriage Assimilation," Jewish Telegraphic Agency, June 20, 1979, https://www.jta.org/1979/06/20/archive/orthodox-group-forms-unit-to-combat-intermarriage-assimilation.

2. Summaries and discussions of the survey, along with the questionnaire and data sets, are collected at http://www.jewishdatabank.org/Studies/details .cfm?StudyID=305. See, for example, Barry A. Kosmin et al., *Highlights of the CJF 1990 National Jewish Population Survey* (New York: Council of Jewish Federations, 1991).

3. *A Portrait of Jewish Americans: Findings from a Pew Research Center Survey of U.S. Jews* (Washington, DC: Pew Research Center, 2013).

4. Avram Mlotek, "Time to Rethink Our Resistance to Intermarriage," *New York Jewish Week*, June 13, 2017, https://jewishweek.timesofisrael.com/time-to -rethink-our-resistance-to-intermarriage.

5. Adina Lewittes, quoted in Emma Green, "'We're Headed toward One of the Greatest Divisions in the History of the Jewish People,'" *Atlantic*, July 16, 2017, https://www.theatlantic.com/politics/archive/2017/07/intermarriage-conservative -judaism/533637.

6. Rachel Altman, "The New Minority: Jews Who Choose Jews," *Lilith*, Summer 1994.

7. Naomi Schaefer Riley, *'Til Faith Do Us Part: How Interfaith Marriage Is Transforming America* (New York: Oxford University Press, 2013).

8. Robert D. Putnam and David E. Campbell, with Shaylyn Romney Garrett, *American Grace: How Religion Divides and Unites Us* (New York: Simon & Schuster, 2010), 549–50.

9. Green, "'We're Headed.'"

CHAPTER 7: IS THE SYNAGOGUE (AND ALL OTHER JEWISH INSTITUTIONS) REALLY DEAD?

1. Gil Rendle, *Journey in the Wilderness: New Life for Mainline Churches* (Nashville, TN: Abingdon Press, 2010).

CHAPTER 8: ISRAEL: INGATHERING OR IMPEDIMENT?

1. Stated by the character Warren in the poem, "The Death of the Hired Man." Robert Frost, "The Death of the Hired Man," in *Robert Frost: Collected Poems, Prose, & Plays*, ed. Richard Poirier and Mark Richardson (New York: Library of America, 1995), 40–45.

2. Benjamin Netanyahu, "PM Netanyahu's Remarks at the Start of the Weekly Cabinet Meeting," Israel Ministry of Foreign Affairs, September 3, 2017, http:// mfa.gov.il/MFA/PressRoom/2017/Pages/PM-Netanyahu%27s-remarks-at-the

-start-of-the-weekly-Cabinet-meeting-3-September-2017.aspx; Shira Rubin, "Israel to African Refugees: You're Not Welcome Here," *USA Today*, November 2, 2017, https://www.usatoday.com/story/news/world/2017/11/02/israel-african -refugees-youre-not-welcome/804628001.

3. Amir Tibon, "'Pathetic': U.S. Jewish Leader Blasts Netanyahu and His Government for 'Hate Speech' against Reform Jews," *Ha'aretz*, July 5, 2018, https://www.haaretz.com/us-news/.premium-u-s-jewish-leader-blasts-gov-t -for-hate-speech-against-reform-jews-1.6245696.

4. Seth Farber, "Fighting for Judaism in the Jewish State," *New York Times*, August 1, 2018, https://www.nytimes.com/2018/08/01/opinion/israel-judaism -weddings.html.

5. William Galston, "The Fracturing of the Jewish People," *Wall Street Journal*, June 12, 2018, https://www.wsj.com/articles/the-fracturing-of-the-jewish -people-1528844625.

6. Gideon Levy, "One State, One Vote," *Ha'aretz*, July 8, 2018, https://www .haaretz.com/opinion/.premium-one-state-one-vote-1.6246981.

7. See, for example, Daniel Bar-Tal, *The Massada Syndrome: A Case of Central Belief* (Tel Aviv: International Center for Peace in the Middle East, 1983).

8. Alan Elsner, "American Jews Overwhelmingly Back Two-State Solution," *Huffington Post*, November 5, 2014, https://www.huffingtonpost.com/alan -elsner/american-jews-overwhelmin_b_6107430.html.

9. Amanda Borschel-Dan, "Angry US Donor Wants to Issue 'a Wake-Up Call,' Isn't Planning to Pull His Israel Funding," *Times of Israel*, July 3, 2017, https://www.timesofisrael.com/angry-us-donor-wants-to-issue-a-wake-up-call -isnt-planning-to-pull-his-israel-funding.

CHAPTER 9: AN OPEN DOOR:
THE "NEW" JEWISH COMMUNITY

1. Terry Bookman and William Kahn, *This House We Build: Lessons for Healthy Synagogues and the People Who Dwell There* (Lanham, MD: Rowman & Littlefield, 2007).

2. Sidney Schwarz, *Jewish Megatrends: Charting the Course of the American Jewish Future* (Woodstock, VT: Jewish Lights, 2013).

3. Eugene B. Borowitz, *Renewing the Covenant: A Theology for the Postmodern Jew* (Philadelphia: Jewish Publication Society, 1996).

4. Joel Lurie Grishaver and Beth Huppin, *Tzedakah, Gemilut Chasadim and Ahavah: A Manual for World Repair* (Denver, CO: A.R.E. Publishing, 1983).

5. My thinking on community has been largely influenced by Rabbi Borowitz as well as the lectures and work of Peter Block, collected in Peter Block, *Community: The Structure of Belonging* (San Francisco, CA: Berrett-Koehler, 2009).

BEYOND SURVIVAL: AN AFTERWORD

1. Howard Bogot, *To See the World through Jewish Eyes: Guidelines for the Primary Years* (New York: UAHC, 1982).

2. BrainyQuote, https://www.brainyquote.com/quotes/winston_churchill_103739.

3. Martin Luther King Jr., "Remaining Awake through a Great Revolution" (commencement address, Oberlin College, Oberlin, OH, June 14, 1965), http://www2.oberlin.edu/external/EOG/BlackHistoryMonth/MLK/Comm Address.html.

Bibliography

Allen, Adina. "'Is, Was, Will Be.'" *Sh'ma Now: A Journal of Jewish Sensibilities*, February 12, 2017. https://forward.com/shma-now/chidush/362685/39-is -was-will-be39.

Altman, Rachel. "The New Minority: Jews Who Choose Jews." *Lilith*, Summer 1994.

Arendt, Hannah. *The Origins of Totalitarianism*. New York: Harcourt, Brace, 1951.

Bar-Tal, Daniel. *The Massada Syndrome: A Case of Central Belief*. Tel Aviv: International Center for Peace in the Middle East, 1983.

Bennhold, Katrin. "One Legacy of Merkel? Angry East German Men Fueling the Far Right." *New York Times*, November 5, 2018.

Block, Peter. *Community: The Structure of Belonging*. San Francisco, CA: Berrett-Koehler, 2009.

Bogot, Howard. *To See the World through Jewish Eyes: Guidelines for the Primary Years*. New York: UAHC, 1982.

Bookman, Terry, and William Kahn. *This House We Build: Lessons for Healthy Synagogues and the People Who Dwell There*. Lanham, MD: Rowman & Littlefield, 2007.

Borowitz, Eugene B. *Renewing the Covenant: A Theology for the Postmodern Jew*. Philadelphia: Jewish Publication Society, 1996.

Borschel-Dan, Amanda. "Angry US Donor Wants to Issue 'a Wake-Up Call,' Isn't Planning to Pull His Israel Funding." *Times of Israel*, July 3, 2017. https:// www.timesofisrael.com/angry-us-donor-wants-to-issue-a-wake-up-call-isnt -planning-to-pull-his-israel-funding.

———. "Will New Conversion Bill Help 400,000 Israelis of 'No Religion'? Not Likely." *Times of Israel*, April 24, 2018. https://www.timesofisrael.com/will -new-conversion-bill-help-400000-israelis-of-no-religion-not-likely.

Burg, Avraham. *The Holocaust Is Over: We Must Rise from Its Ashes.* New York: Palgrave Macmillan, 2008.

Burnett, Dean. *Idiot Brain: What Your Head Is Really Up To.* New York: Norton, 2016.

Covey, Stephen. *The 7 Habits of Highly Effective People.* New York: Simon & Schuster, 1989.

Davidson, Steven. "How Much Do Top Jewish Non-profit Leaders Make?" *Forward*, December 11, 2017. https://forward.com/news/388240/how-much -do-top-jewish-non-profit-leaders-make.

Devir, Nathan P. *New Children of Israel: Emerging Jewish Communities in an Era of Globalization.* Salt Lake City: University of Utah Press, 2017.

Douthat, Ross. "The Jewish Crossroads." *New York Times*, August 4, 2018. https://www.nytimes.com/2018/08/04/opinion/sunday/steven-m-cohen-jew ish-crossroads.html.

Eglash, Ruth. "A 70-Year-Old Mystery: Yemini Jews Say Young Relatives Were Stolen in Israel." *Washington Post*, August 8, 2016. https://www.wash ingtonpost.com/world/middle_east/a-70-year-old-mystery-yemeni-jews-say -young-relatives-were-stolen-in-israel/2016/08/05/385c8d4f-0831-48a9-aaba -a3c9ff3c275c_story.html?utm_term=.d93300ce41f5.

Elsner, Alan. "American Jews Overwhelmingly Back Two-State Solution." *Huff- ington Post*, November 5, 2014. https://www.huffingtonpost.com/alan-elsner/ american-jews-overwhelmin_b_6107430.html.

Farber, Seth. "Fighting for Judaism in the Jewish State." *New York Times*, Au- gust 1, 2018. https://www.nytimes.com/2018/08/01/opinion/israel-judaism -weddings.html.

Faulkner, William. *Requiem for a Nun.* New York: Vintage, 2011.

Fisher, Roger, and William Ury. *Getting to Yes: Negotiating Agreement without Giving In.* Rev. ed. New York: Penguin, 2001.

Foer, Jonathan Safran. *Here I Am.* New York: Farrar, Straus & Giroux, 2016.

Frost, Robert. "The Death of the Hired Man." In *Robert Frost: Collected Poems, Prose, & Plays*, edited by Richard Poirier and Mark Richardson, 40–45. New York: Library of America, 1995.

Fuchs, Hadas, and Gilad Brand. "Education and Employment Trends among Ethiopian Israelis." Taub Center for Social Policy Studies in Israel, June 2015. http://taubcenter.org.il/wp-content/files_mf/ethiopianeducationandemploy ment2015english.pdf.

Galston, William. "The Fracturing of the Jewish People." *Wall Street Journal*, June 12, 2018. https://www.wsj.com/articles/the-fracturing-of-the-jewish-peo ple-1528844625.

Goldman, Ari. "Dalai Lama Meets Jews from Four Major Branches." *New York Times*, September 26, 1989, B4. https://www.nytimes.com/1989/09/26/nyre gion/dalai-lama-meets-jews-from-4-major-branches.html.

Green, Emma. "'We're Headed toward One of the Greatest Divisions in the History of the Jewish People.'" *Atlantic*, July 16, 2017. https://www.theatlan tic.com/politics/archive/2017/07/intermarriage-conservative-judaism/533637.

Grishaver, Joel Lurie, and Beth Huppin. *Tzedakah, Gemilut Chasadim and Aha-vah: A Manual for World Repair*. Denver, CO: A.R.E. Publishing, 1983.

"Iran: We Will Help 'Cut Out the Cancer of Israel.'" *Telegraph*, February 3, 2012. https://www.telegraph.co.uk/news/worldnews/middleeast/iran/9059179/Iran -We-will-help-cut-out-the-cancer-of-Israel.html.

Johnson, Spencer. *Who Moved My Cheese? An Amazing Way to Deal with Change in Your Work and in Your Life*. New York: Putnam, 1998.

J Street. *The 2018 Jewish Vote: National Post-Election Survey*. J Street Elec-tion Night Survey Presentation, November 2018. https://jstreet.org/wp-con tent/uploads/2018/11/J-Street-2018-Election-Night-Survey-Presentation -110818.pdf.

King, Martin Luther, Jr. "Remaining Awake through a Great Revolution." Commencement address, Oberlin College, Oberlin, OH, June 14, 1965. http://www2.oberlin.edu/external/EOG/BlackHistoryMonth/MLK/Comm Address.html.

Kosmin, Barry A., et al. *Highlights of the CJF 1990 National Jewish Population Survey*. New York: Council of Jewish Federations, 1991.

Kovel, Joel. *White Racism: A Psychohistory*. New York: Pantheon, 1970.

Kurzban, Robert, John Tooby, and Leda Cosmides. "Can Race Be Erased? Co-alitional Computation and Social Categorization." *Proceedings of the National Academy of Sciences* 98, no. 26 (December 18, 2001): 15387–92. https://doi .org/10.1073/pnas.251541498.

Landrieu, Mitch. "On the Removal of Four Confederate Monuments in New Orleans." Speech, Gallier Hall, New Orleans, LA, May 19, 2017.

Levy, Gideon. "One State, One Vote." *Ha'aretz*, July 8, 2018. https://www .haaretz.com/opinion/.premium-one-state-one-vote-1.6246981.

Marcus, Jacob Rader. *The Jew in the Medieval World: A Sourcebook, 315–1791*. 2nd ed. Cincinnati, OH: Hebrew Union College Press, 1999.

Milgrom, Genie. *My 15 Grandmothers*. Lexington, KY: G. Milgrom, 2012.

Mlotek, Avram. "Time to Rethink Our Resistance to Intermarriage." *New York Jewish Week*, June 13, 2017. https://jewishweek.timesofisrael.com/time-to -rethink-our-resistance-to-intermarriage.

Netanyahu, Benjamin. "PM Netanyahu's Remarks at the Start of the Weekly Cabinet Meeting." Israel Ministry of Foreign Affairs, September 3, 2017.

http://mfa.gov.il/MFA/PressRoom/2017/Pages/PM-Netanyahu%27s-re
marks-at-the-start-of-the-weekly-Cabinet-meeting-3-September-2017.aspx.

"Orthodox Group Forms Unit to Combat Intermarriage Assimilation." Jewish
Telegraphic Agency, June 20, 1979. https://www.jta.org/1979/06/20/archive/
orthodox-group-forms-unit-to-combat-intermarriage-assimilation.

Parhar, Gurdeep. "Fixing Racism." Lecture, TEDxStanleyPark, Vancouver, BC,
May 28, 2016. https://www.tedxstanleypark.com/speakers/2016-2.

*A Portrait of Jewish Americans: Findings from a Pew Research Center Survey of U.S.
Jews.* Washington, DC: Pew Research Center, 2013.

Putnam, Robert D. *Bowling Alone: The Collapse and Revival of American Community.* New York: Simon & Schuster, 2000.

Putnam, Robert D., and David E. Campbell, with Shaylyn Romney Garrett.
American Grace: How Religion Divides and Unites Us. New York: Simon &
Schuster, 2010.

Puzzo, Dante A. "Racism and the Western Tradition." *Journal of the History of Ideas* 25, no. 4 (October–December 1964): 579–86. https://doi
.org/10.2307/2708188.

Regalado, Antonio. "2017 Was the Year Consumer DNA Testing Blew Up."
MIT Technology Review, February 12, 2018. https://www.technologyreview
.com/s/610233/2017-was-the-year-consumer-dna-testing-blew-up.

Rendle, Gil. *Journey in the Wilderness: New Life for Mainline Churches.* Nashville,
TN: Abingdon Press, 2010.

Riley, Naomi Schaefer. *'Til Faith Do Us Part: How Interfaith Marriage Is Transforming America* (New York: Oxford University Press, 2013).

Ross, Lesli Koppelman. "The Importance of Remembering." My Jewish Learning,
https://www.myjewishlearning.com/article/the-importance-of-remembering.

Rubin, Shira. "Israel to African Refugees: You're Not Welcome Here." *USA Today*,
November 2, 2017. https://www.usatoday.com/story/news/world/2017/11/02/
israel-african-refugees-youre-not-welcome/804628001.

Sales, Ben. "New President Seeks to Cure 'Epidemic' of Racism." *Times of Israel*,
October 24, 2015. https://www.timesofisrael.com/new-president-seeks-to
-cure-disease-of-racism.

Scholem, Gershom. *The Messianic Idea in Judaism and Other Essays on Jewish
Spirituality.* New York: Schocken Books, 1971.

Schwarz, Sidney. *Finding a Spiritual Home: How a New Generation of Jews Can
Transform the American Synagogue.* Woodstock, VT: Jewish Lights, 2000.

———. *Jewish Megatrends: Charting the Course of the American Jewish Future.*
Woodstock, VT: Jewish Lights, 2013.

Seifert, Charles C. *The Negro's or Ethiopian's Contribution to Art.* BCP Pamphlet.
Baltimore, MD: Black Classic Press, 1986. Originally published in 1938.

Selby, Gary S. *Martin Luther King and the Rhetoric of Freedom.* Waco, TX: Baylor University Press, 2009.

Selengut, Suzanne. "The Converso Comeback." *Tablet Magazine,* October 17, 2017. https://www.tabletmag.com/jewish-life-and-religion/246057/the-converso-comeback.

State of Israel. Declaration of the Establishment of the State of Israel, May 14, 1948.

Talk of the Nation. Hosted by Neal Conan. NPR, December 8, 2008.

Tepper, Greg. "Israel a 'Cancerous Tumor' and Middle East's Biggest Problem, Iranian Supreme Leader Says." *Times of Israel,* August 19, 2012. http://www.timesofisrael.com/khamenei-israeli-a-malignant-zionist-tumor.

Tibon, Amir. "'Pathetic': U.S. Jewish Leader Blasts Netanyahu and His Government for 'Hate Speech' against Reform Jews." *Ha'aretz,* July 5, 2018. https://www.haaretz.com/us-news.premium-u-s-jewish-leader-blasts-gov-t-for-hate-speech-against-reform-jews-1.6245696.

Watanabe, Teresa. "Nation of Islam Leader Raises the Loyalty Issue." *Los Angeles Times,* August 12, 2000. http://articles.latimes.com/2000/aug/12/news/mn-3360.

Weber, Max. *The Protestant Ethic and the Spirit of Capitalism.* Translated by Talcott Parsons. New York: Scribner, 1958.

Index

167